W9-CCM-500

"Some experiences we go through are made more difficult by fame and fortune. *Believing in Magic* is an example that one's true treasure lies in faith, tenacity, and a sense of one's own purpose in life."

—Courtney B. Vance and Angela Bassett

"In 1991, Cookie and Earvin (Magic) Johnson came to West Angeles Church amid a crisis greater than most couples ever experience. It has been an honor to know them, serve them, and love them and their family unconditionally as they have journeyed from then until now. We are convinced that this exciting and well-written story will touch and thrill the hearts of many for years to come."

—Bishop Charles and "Lady Mae" Blake,
West Angeles Church of God in Christ

"Cookie has never been one to seek the spotlight, and I'm thrilled that she is now sharing her story. Her beautifully written book will inspire and empower others to overcome any challenges in their lives. Cookie Johnson believes in Magic and I believe in her."

—Robin Roberts

"A poignant account of their time together. This book answers many of the whys of their relationship, but more important it shows Cookie's strength, tenacity, intelligence, and sheer will to raise her family, live an authentic life, and support her soulmate. A must read!"

—Tonya and Dave Winfield

"Cookie is an amazing woman! Her family's journey has been truly *inspiring* and *magical*. . . . We love and admire you, big sis and big bro!"

—LL Cool J and Simone I. Smith

Believing
in Magic

· · · · · · · ·

Cookie Johnson
with Denene Millner

HOWARD BOOKS
An Imprint of Simon & Schuster, Inc.

New York   Nashville   London   Toronto   Sydney   New Delhi

Howard Books
An Imprint of Simon & Schuster, Inc.
1230 Avenue of the Americas
New York, NY 10020

First Howard Books hardcover edition September 2016

HOWARD and colophon are trademarks of Simon & Schuster, Inc.

For information about special discounts for bulk purchases, please contact Simon &
Schuster Special Sales at 1-866-506-1949 or business@simonandschuster.com.

The Simon & Schuster Speakers Bureau can bring authors to your live event. For more
information or to book an event, contact the Simon & Schuster Speakers Bureau at
1-866-248-3049 or visit our website at www.simonspeakers.com.

Interior design by Jaime Putorti

Manufactured in the United States of America

10   9   8   7   6   5   4   3   2   1

Library of Congress Cataloging-in-Publication Data is available.

ISBN 978-1-5011-2515-7
ISBN 978-1-5011-2518-8 (ebook)

I dedicate this book to God.

Without Him, my obstacles would have been unconquerable. Always, He is by my side, guiding, directing, and carrying me when I cannot stand on my own.

"For God is the author and finisher of our faith."

—Hebrews 12:2

· Contents ·

"I'm coming home early because I have to tell you something," he said.

I rested the cold phone receiver against my cheek as I stared at the TV, confused, alternately searching for my husband's face and his number—32—among the sea of yellow-and-purple jerseys darting across the screen. I'd just settled into the chaise in our family room, a big bowl of popcorn in my lap, with my girlfriend, Nicole, by my side. The two of us had been laughing and talking about everything and nothing, really, waiting for the televised game to start when I got his phone call. Earvin, the basketball legend known around the world as Magic Johnson, the point guard who'd led the Los Angeles Lakers to five NBA championships, was supposed to be in Salt Lake City, warming up for the big preseason game against the Utah Jazz. Instead, he was in a car, heading to the airport, working his way back to LA.

"Why?" I asked. I tightened my grip around the receiver and passed one more nervous look at the television screen and then at Nicole. Just then, a commentator announced that my husband was out sick with the flu. "Are you okay?"

"I have to talk to you, but I'm on my way to the doctor's office right now. I'll tell you what's going on when I get home, Cookie," he said slowly. "I can't tell you over the phone. I'm on my way to you."

Earvin's words—hushed, somber, deliberate—sent a chill creeping over my heart, into the pit of my stomach, through my bones, all the way down to the very tips of my slipper-covered toes. Initially, I didn't know what to make of it. But in the hours it took until he walked through our front door, I'd worked myself into quite a frenzy. My considerations began with illness—maybe he'd broken a bone or tore an ACL or pulled a tendon or gotten some other god-awful career-ending injury. And then I thought that maybe he'd had a run-in with a teammate, or worse, Lakers owner, Jerry Buss, or perhaps the coach, Mike Dunleavy. By the time Nicole said her good-byes and Earvin was just minutes from our home, I was convinced it was divorce—my husband's urgent phone call and unplanned trip home was to tell me he was leaving me. Sounds absurd, sure—particularly since we'd only been married just shy of forty-five short days and were finally, happily, together as husband and wife. Our marital bliss was hard-won, believe me: we'd had a twelve-year, on-again, off-again romance that stretched back to our freshman year at Michigan State University and, somehow, survived a long-distance courtship and two dramatic broken engagements, both of which began with similar cryptic phone calls like the one Earvin had made to me that night. So shaken was I from Earvin's prior wedding hesitancy that even on the day we exchanged our vows, I was a nervous wreck, thinking the man I'd loved for almost half my life would be a runaway groom—so scared to say "I do" that he'd call my phone, like he'd done all too many times before, to tell me that he just couldn't be with me anymore. That his need for independence was stronger than his desire to commit to me. To us.

But, finally, we were in a good place—the very best a couple in love and building a future together could be. Or so I'd thought up until the very moment he made his unexpected, urgent phone call. Our wedding was one made of fairy tales, and we'd had an equally glorious, albeit short, honeymoon in Malibu. Right after that, I tagged along with my new husband to Paris, where he played preseason exhibition games with his teammates during the day and we squeezed in romantic evening walks along the River Seine, the lights of the Eiffel Tower twinkling in the distance. Rounding out our joy: it was there, in this European paradise, that we newlyweds got the incredible news that I was pregnant with our first child together. What could possibly be more perfect? I was his. He was mine. And now, through the consummation of our love—deep, precious, pure—new life was to be.

We were beyond ecstatic, of course, but Earvin's jam-packed basketball schedule would leave little time for us to celebrate; only days after a drugstore pregnancy test revealed the incredible news, we all flew back as a team to Los Angeles, and I was off to see the ob-gyn while Earvin headed to Salt Lake City for another preseason game against the Utah Jazz.

Salt Lake City is where I expected him to be. But instead, he was on the phone, telling me he was heading to Los Angeles with bad news. I laughed a little. "Well, it couldn't be *that* bad," I said, shifting in my chair. "What's wrong with you . . . do you have AIDS or something?"

Earvin didn't answer.

And so for more than an hour, I imagined my new husband walking through our front door, papers in hand, demanding a divorce. I could barely think straight as I considered what might have gone wrong and all that a breakup would entail: What would happen to our family? Would I raise our baby alone? Would I have to move back to Toledo? Find a new job? How would I explain this to my family? Our friends? How many different ways would we be talked about in gossip columns from Los Angeles to New York? What could I have possibly done to lose my husband so quickly? So decisively?

The moment I heard the turn of the knob to the front door, I rushed from our family room into the foyer and stood there, anxious for my husband to come to me. Lon, Earvin's agent, walked in first, red-faced and leaden. Earvin, a massive man whose six feet, nine inches of lean muscle and brawn usually made him appear like a superhero standing there in our doorway, looked . . . small. Blank. Broken.

Our eyes locked; a rush of adrenaline forced a dull thud of pain to the base of my skull and a bitter taste into the back of my throat. Something was wrong. Terribly wrong. Worse than any breakup. More devastating than any of the scenarios I'd conjured up in my mind. My husband walked toward me, took my hand in his, and slowly marched me back into the den where I'd nervously waited for him. The two of us sat at the foot of our huge chaise longue and, instinctively, I held my breath as I waited for the words that would change our lives in ways I never once imagined.

My husband is HIV-positive—that's the part of my story you already know. But I've never revealed exactly how it felt to have my college sweetheart come home that evening, cup his face in his hands, and utter a sentence that shook us both to our core. I haven't told you just how frightened I was during the ten days I waited to hear whether my unborn child and I were infected. I've never talked about the mix of emotions that coursed through my body as Earvin locked himself in a room and called the long list of women with whom he'd been intimate. I haven't spoken of the night that he and I got down on our knees and cried out to God, or the morning we awakened to realize our nightmare was real. I've never shared all the reasons that I stayed with Earvin, or the time, years later, when we nearly left each other. Until now, the world has never heard the full account of my life with Earvin.

After his November 1991 announcement to the world that he'd acquired the virus that causes AIDS and was retiring from basketball, I don't think many people believed my husband's life would go on for much longer. When I look back on it now, even I wasn't sure what the next days would hold for us. After you get a diagnosis like HIV (human immunodeficiency virus), you stop thinking much about the past or the future. The news shocks you right into the present tense, and the only way you can survive is to breathe your way through this moment. And then the next. And then each one that follows.

The news shocks you right into the present tense, and the only way you can survive is to breathe your way through this moment. And then the next.

I think God is being merciful by allowing us to experience only what's right in front of us. The night my husband told me he had the virus that causes AIDS (acquired immunodeficiency syndrome), I didn't know how his story would end. Or mine. Or that of our unborn child. Neither did he. But ever the point guard, Earvin assessed the court and tried to call the shots. "I understand if you want to leave me," he said, holding me at arm's length as we each wiped our tears. "Because I'm now turning your life upside down."

I snatched my body from his grip and instinctively rubbed my belly. Life was there. Life was us. Right there, in that very moment, I could not imagine taking so much as another breath without Earvin in my life and me in his—the two of us, arm in arm, going to war. This was my husband. And it was not his fight alone. Frankly, I couldn't believe that he'd fix his mouth to suggest that I, his wife, leave him there in that midnight hour, in that darkness, alone. "'Til death do us part" meant something to me when we stood before our friends and our families and our God to claim our forever. That he dared question my loyalty and our resolve as a couple angered me. So much so that I hauled off and slapped his face.

"We're going to beat this together," I said, seething. And then I ordered him to do what I'd done practically my entire life whenever life's adversities made clear that I needed the strength of something so much bigger than me. "Let's get on our knees and pray."

And that's what we did.

This much I know to be true: in that moment, I was sure of the things I'd always clung to. My unshakeable faith and my trust that God would see me through. My family. My friendships. And a love for Earvin that would be tested time and time again in the twenty-five years to follow.

Chapter One

Meeting Magic

I had no clue who Earvin "Magic" Johnson was when I got my acceptance letter to Michigan State University. I was a high school cheerleader, yes, and had enough of a working knowledge about basketball that I knew the difference between a free throw and a three-point shot, but really, outside of waving my pom-poms for the Chadsey High Explorers, I didn't pay any mind to the game or the athletes who excelled in it. Here's what was on my mind: working, applying to college, securing federal grants to pay my tuition, and figuring out if I wanted to be bothered anymore with Brent, my high school sweetheart who reveled in his self-importance as the lead of a local band and also took great pleasure in finding ways to try to make me jealous of his popularity and all that came with being a small-time Detroit celebrity, at least in his mind.

What Brent refused to grasp about Earleatha Kelly was that I was much too independent and focused to be moved by his success or pressed by his constant attempts to goad a brawl between some random girl in his band and me. I am, after all, the middle child of Earl and Cora Kelly, two no-nonsense southerners from Huntsville, Alabama, who loved hard, fought for our very existence when they moved us up North, looking for a sound living wage as part of the Great Migration, and broke up dramatically years later, leaving me, my sister, Pat, and my little brother, Harold, to figure out really quickly how to do for ourselves while they struggled to hold on to their humanity postdivorce. When my father moved out, my mother was suddenly charged with taking care of herself and her three kids sans the financial stability that came with a marriage, which meant that for the first time in her life as a parent, she was a single mom and the primary provider. As her role changed, so did ours. Her focus was keeping a roof over our heads and food in our bellies—survival mode. Everything else, well, we quickly figured out how to do for ourselves. That was our reality. It was nothing for me, after cheering at a game, to hop on a bus way across town at 9:00 p.m. and find my way home. It was very clear to me, as it was to my sister, that my mother was available if we needed help, but she was to be tapped only if there was a problem. Otherwise, we were in charge of our own destinies. So while she toiled in the women's fashion department at J. C. Penney, we kids got busy chipping in with the care and upkeep of our home and ourselves. Between my sister, Pat, and me, I think we did a fine job: we got ourselves to school and activities, we disciplined our little brother and made sure he got his homework done, and any extra money we needed, we earned it for ourselves. I'll never forget how my mother sat me down in my senior year and had an honest, straightforward heart-to-heart with me about my high school graduation activities and what she could and couldn't realistically afford to finance. There was the fee for the cap and gown, and the senior trip and prom, and, of course, the high school ring, which I wanted most of all.

"I can't afford all that," my mother said candidly one evening. I could tell she was hurt by this. "I can afford some, maybe the senior trip and the cap and gown. But the rest, I can't handle right now."

"I understand," I said. "It's fine. I'll go get a job."

And that's what I did.

I relished in that autonomy—that control over my own destiny. Indeed, I think that my mother's hands-off approach to parenting not only made me grow up but also taught me rather early that my happiness was up to me—that it was,

My happiness was up to me—that it was, and always will be, in my own hands.

and always will be, in my own hands. I'm grateful to her for that.

My own personal triumph was applying for and getting accepted into college, and earning the money I needed to pay for it, all on my own. My mother was surprised and a smidge impressed by my tenacity.

"Mom, I'm going to go to college," I said to her one Saturday evening after she'd come in from a long day's work. She was helping me clear the dinner table. "I'm doing my applications. I'm going to go."

My mother looked at me, perplexed and definitely a bit worried. "I don't know how you're gonna pay for that," she said quietly. "I can't afford it."

I rushed into my room and gathered up the paperwork that, with the help of my boyfriend's mother, I'd been filling out for weeks. I pushed the papers in her general direction. My mother carefully looked them over and then laid the papers on the table. "That's good, Cookie. Real good."

My move to apply to college displayed for my mother rather early on that, by action and deed, I was truly independent and capable of taking the reins of my own future; her worry over how I'd get to college quickly morphed into joy. But while my mother was proud of my self-sufficiency, my boyfriend felt differently about it. It would drive him absolutely batty to know that if I needed anything, I had no problem going out there and getting it on my own— an independence that effectively crushed his attempts to control me.

For sure, Brent, whom I dated in my senior year, fought against who I was becoming from the very start. Perhaps I was too naïve to understand it back then, but now I recognize that he'd spent a year grooming me to be his own personal groupie—the girl who would follow behind him, shower him with adoration, and let him run roughshod over our relationship while I stood dutifully by, supporting his burgeoning career and cheering him on. It worked, I guess, for a while; chalk that up to immaturity. But the moment that I started working and got really focused on graduating high school and getting myself off to college, I became a problem for him. And he began to work overtime to keep me in my place the best way he knew how: by manipulating with jealousy. A girl who played in his band was his most perfect pawn.

I saw the way she looked at him—the short skirts she wore and the mid-drift shirts. I hated the way she popped her gum while she rubbed his shoulders and his back and the way she would bend over suggestively when she knew he'd be walking by. One evening when the band was warming up for a show, I followed her into the club's bathroom and worked up enough nerve to confront her. "Brent is my boyfriend," I said, looking her straight in the eyes.

She was nonplussed. "Well, I don't know what you're talking about," she said slyly. "But if he likes it, I don't know why you're talking to me."

I couldn't believe it: in one sentence, she'd both denied and copped to flirting with my boyfriend. But she was right, and I'd learned a valuable lesson from her in that short exchange: it wasn't the woman's actions I needed to be concerned about. It was my man's reaction to them, how he would choose to move forward with our relationship once confronted, and the care he would take with my feelings and respecting me while we worked through the issues at hand.

Let's just say that Brent failed miserably on all fronts. Rather than send his "work girlfriend" packing, he let her keep playing in the band, instead choosing to suffocate me with demands that I stop working, forget about going away to college and attend school at a small, local institution, and spend the rest of my days following him all around town. His foolish mandates and my refusal to capitulate came to a head one evening when I stopped by his home with a particularly challenging college application his mother had agreed to help me fill out. "Why are you even applying for school?" Brent asked, seething. "You don't need to go to college."

I looked up from my paperwork and tossed a confused look his way. He knew full well that my dream was to be a buyer in the fashion industry and that the only way I could do that was to get a degree in my chosen field. Still, here he was, making the argument for laying up under him for the rest of my life. "Uh, yeah, I do have to go to school," I said. "That's kind of what I *want* to do."

Back then, as I am today, I could be quite passive; there's not a lot that can really shake me. But when I'm passionate about something—when it's important to me, and I've decided that you are an impediment to what it is I'm trying to do—you could be screaming your request through a megaphone directly into my ear, rimmed with emotions worthy of an Oscar, and your words won't matter. "This isn't about you," I insisted. "I'm doing this for me."

For a while, Brent laid off trying to convince me not to go to college, but the moment he found out I'd accepted an offer from Michigan State, he lost it. "You're going to Michigan State?" he asked.

"Yes!" I said excitedly. "It's such a good program for retailing. It's perfect."

My enthusiasm only made him more agitated. "What's wrong with the community college here in town?" he asked. "I don't see why you have to go all the way to Lansing to study what you can learn right here."

"Michigan State is a great opportunity for me," I answered slowly, wrinkling my brow. "Plus, I got a bunch of grants and everything. I can't turn this down."

"I don't want you going to that school," he said angrily.

"What are you talking about?" I insisted. "Why not?"

"'Cause you're gonna go up there and you're gonna meet that Magic Johnson guy."

"Who?" I asked, genuinely confused. "Who are you talking about?"

"Earvin Johnson," Brent said, exasperated. "Magic Johnson!"

Now, to understand Brent's concern, one must understand the phenomenon that was Magic Johnson. He was a high school basketball miracle from Lansing, Michigan, who lived up to the nickname given him by a sportswriter after a game in which he scored a triple double: 36 points, 18 rebounds, and 16 assists. Anyone who followed high school basketball knew that his going to Michigan State was a coup for the university, which would no doubt see its fair share of NCAA championship action with the young basketball wonder, who graduated with two All-State selections and a spot on the 1977 McDonald's All-American team. There was no doubt in the mind of anyone paying attention that Earvin "Magic" Johnson was going to be a big deal, not only on campus at Michigan State, but eventually in the NBA, and that fact had Brent, a former high school basketball player, anxious. How, after all, would he be able to stop his inexperienced but ambitious girlfriend from falling under the spell of the most promising baller out of the entire state of Michigan? How would he be able to control me a full hour and a half away from his clutches, particularly when a man, presumably more successful than he was, was within reach?

Brent was so serious about this scenario. I thought he'd lost his mind, and I had no problem telling him so. "So what you're saying is not, 'Cookie, don't move because I'll miss you.' You don't want me to go to school and work toward my dream because of some guy I don't even know?" I yelled. "You're talking so crazy right now!"

Days later, Brent slept with that girl from his band and came back to tell me about it—like a chapter straight out of the player's book of manipulation. I'm guessing he thought that I would stay in Detroit to try to save our relationship or something.

He was so wrong about many things, this one included. But as nutty as I pegged Brent to be, I didn't think for even a single second that his prediction of a union between Earvin and me would come true.

Silly me.

• Big Man on Campus •

It didn't hit me until I was standing in the parking lot in front of my dorm at Michigan State, bawling and waving goodbye after my father's little pickup truck, that I'd left home—that I was on my own. My mother and I never had a conversation about the transition, and we certainly didn't fret over it. She is the kind of person who goes with the moment, and, perhaps by extension, I am this way, too. So it didn't occur to either of us to discuss the physical, emotional, or mental transition that came with taking that first unsure step into adulthood. I was all sunshine and rainbows tucked between my mother and father during the hour-and-a-half ride from Detroit to Lansing, reveling in the first short reunion of my parents since their divorce. But the saddest, scariest moment of my life up until then hit me when the two of them slowly pulled down the road, away from me. It was the tears glistening on my mother's cheeks that put me over the edge.

Still, the excitement of being on campus on my own settled in just as quickly. Within ten minutes of that most devastating good-bye, I was in my dorm room, giggling and making plans with my girlfriends, including my roommate Adrianne, who was my best friend and fellow cheerleader from back in Detroit. Adrianne had been in the same tailoring program as I had at our high school, and she, too, had applied and was accepted into Michigan State's fashion program, with the hope of becoming a buyer. I don't know how our friendship survived through high school and college; we'd had our fair share of fall-outs and silences over the years—the natural ebb and flow of a sound relationship, I guess. But we made it through and remain steadfast friends even to this day. Adrianne would become an important piece in our game of survival at Michigan State, which, with our entry in the fall of 1977, was experiencing one of the first integrated campuses since a federal grant program aimed at helping black students afford tuition at predominately white colleges and universities across the country went into effect. We had to stick together—had no other choice. Our numbers were small, but resistance to our presence from white students, faculty, and staff was palpable. Nobody did anything untoward; there weren't any blatant incidents of racial violence or name-calling. It was just a vibe, a feeling we all got as we navigated the campus and the college experience. For me, it was especially noticeable in my dealings with the counselors, the people charged with guiding me through the maze of class requirements and scheduling. Questions were met with indifference; answers, what few there'd been, were stiff and sterile. I would say, "I'm having a hard time with this particular class, and I don't know what to do," and they'd look at me, unmoved, and say, "You can drop it if you want to, but if you drop it, you will lose the credit." There was no figuring out which courses would make a better fit and still meet requirements—no road map for negotiating the tricky terrain of matriculating into life on a campus where we were but specks of unwanted pepper in a grand bowl of white milk. The most effort my specific counselor ever extended was the energy it took for her to push a standard schedule of class requirements for my major across her desk. The first time she did it, I stared at the paper, overwhelmed by its contents. "Okay," I said, looking at the paper and then back at her, "based on my schedule, I guess I have to figure this out."

"You'll figure it out," she said, sitting back in her chair, signaling the end of our meeting.

This was nothing short of cultural shock for me. After all, I grew up in Detroit. Motor City. Motown. Black folk. Outside of our relatively integrated school, I don't think I ever saw white people, much less lived among them, and that's the truth. I do believe I may have gasped when I ran into a white girl in the dorm bathroom; she looked at me, too, like, "Oh God, you're living on our floor?" It was the same look, that same vibe, I got from all too many on that campus—from the professors on down. It was traumatic—made me feel less than. And that was a tough thing to negotiate at age eighteen, particularly without the guidance of my parents, who'd never been to college and couldn't warn me about the land mines I'd face in such a volatile environment. It didn't help, either, that I arrived ill prepared for the academic workload. Granted, I graduated with honors from my high school, but it was a school that focused on trades—tailoring, woodshop, commercial food service, and other practical skills that were meant to help students leave school and get jobs, not necessarily college educations. As smart as I thought I was, I wasn't particularly well-read, hadn't been introduced to advanced math concepts or science theory, or encouraged to consider any kind of deep analysis of history and politics. Rarely did we write. My lack in those advanced curriculum areas made it easy for me to fall behind, yes, but also helped sustain the preconceived beliefs of the professors and counselors who were hostile to our presence and made clear they didn't think we were up to snuff. Fighting against that attitude was, perhaps, the most challenging part of attending a predominately white institution, particularly as part of the first generation of blacks to integrate the campuses.

Thank God, we had a black student union that gave us access to older students who were happy to advise us on what we needed to know to survive there, and the black Greek fraternities and sororities did a fine job of contributing to our social and cultural experiences on campus. Between the two, all hope wasn't lost.

In our first days on campus, Adrianne, another friend, Penny, and a few new friends who hailed from Detroit and I made quick work of running roughshod through that campus. We'd meet in our all-girls' dorm, which we not so affectionately nicknamed "the Nunnery," and download on what we'd be getting into, which boys we were interested in getting to know a little better, and how we would take special care to not be the social misfits among the larger group of black misfits on our mostly homogenous campus. Of course, among our small group, Earvin Johnson was a frequent topic of conversation; a few of the girls were far more aware of who he was than I was, and they often plotted out ways they'd get his attention. We were hardly a week into the first semester when one girl made her move. Rolling about six deep, we were making our way to an intramural basketball game across campus when one of my new friends spotted Earvin walking back across campus to his dorm.

"Oh my God, that's him!" she exclaimed.

I was slightly rattled by her enthusiasm. "Who?" I asked, aloof and oblivious to who was strolling our way.

"Magic Johnson," my friends said, practically in three-part harmony.

I squinted and cocked my head to the side. *Oh, wow—so that's him, huh?* I said to myself. By then, I knew full well who he was; one would have had to been blind and deaf not to, especially if you lived in Lansing and particularly if you were on the Michigan

State campus for longer than two seconds. There he was, splayed across the pages of the newspaper and on the lips of all the local radio deejays and pushing basketballs up court on the six o'clock news. Practically every sports journalist and amateur observer was speculating about what his first game would be like and whether he would be a good fit for the team and if he'd live up to his magical nickname. The hype was inescapable. And that had many a Michigan State student, especially the women, in quite the tizzy. Earvin "Magic" Johnson was our campus's most eligible bachelor.

So when we'd spotted Earvin strolling across campus between classes, it made perfect sense that one of my friends, this one particularly bold, would make her move. "I'm going to say hello."

And who were we to stop her? Sure enough, when we were within earshot, she did it: "Hi!" she said in a singsong voice.

"Hi," Earvin said just as easily as our group of giggling girls rolled in his direction. He slowed his stride and stopped directly in front of us. An easy smile spread across his face as each of us introduced ourselves to him.

"So," my bold friend asked, "what you doing now?"

"Oh, I was just heading back to my room. I just had practice," he said.

A few more quick exchanges, and he went his way and we went ours, with my friends practically melting from the interaction. Of course, all that kept running through my mind was, *Huh. So that's who Brent was talking about.* But Adrianne had bigger plans. When we got back to our room, she made it clear that she was going to make magic with Magic.

"Oh my God, he's amazing!" she said later in our dorm room. She twirled onto her bed and sighed. "I'm going to marry him."

We just laughed and laughed behind that proclamation, because, really, what were the chances of any of us getting his attention beyond a quick chat on the campus lawn, much less an invitation to marry Michigan State's star athlete?

Well, if you know Adrianne, you know she's not easily deterred. Her plan: to show up to the men's basketball practices and make googly eyes at Earvin until he noticed her. "You should come with me!" she practically cheered.

"I'm sorry, but I'm going to have to sit those out," I said, shaking my head. I was genuinely perplexed. "Why would you do that?"

"Because I want to see him," she chimed.

"Okay, you're crazy," I said, shaking my head, my brows furrowed. In her mind, prancing on the front row at Earvin's practices made all the sense in the world. I, however, genuinely didn't understand the point of standing around ogling a guy who, because of his fame, likely wouldn't see us or hear any of our voices over the glitz and din created by his own celebrity.

Besides, I didn't have time for watching practices anyway. Academically, I was struggling and already looking at having to take on a tutor and, perhaps, summer classes to maintain a grade-point average that would keep the scholarship money coming. Plus, as a member of the school spirit squad, the Spartan Spirits, I was already spending my fair share of time at the games, face painted, throat sore from yelling, limbs worn out from cheering and waving placards and getting the crowd hyped around our team. I didn't need to be at the practices, too.

And then there was Andy, a guy who was dating a girl who lived upstairs from Adrianne and me. I thought he was cute, and word on campus was that the couple wasn't all that serious, which, in my mind, meant I had a chance. So if there was any guy on whom I was going to focus what little bit of attention I had to offer, it was going to be Andy.

Adrianne was undeterred. About a month into her mission, she rushed into our dorm room one particular afternoon absolutely swooning. "He waved at me!" she said, practically breathless. She jumped onto the bed and giggled while she kicked her feet against the mattress. "I waved, and he waved back!"

I simply laughed. To her, that wave was progress; to me, it was an exercise in futility. I quickly changed the subject. "Everybody's going to Dooley's tonight," I said as I arranged my books and some schoolwork on my desk. "I think Andy might be going, too, which should make this an interesting night. You coming?"

Adrianne's face dropped. Unbeknownst to me, she was going through some things with the guy she was dealing with at the time, and she didn't feel like seeing him that night, so she decided to stay home. Far be it from me, though, to pass up on a good time.

A few hours later, my friend Becky and I walked into Dooley's and standing right there on the other side of the entrance was none other than Earvin Johnson and a friend of his, Jay.

"Oh my God, it's them," Becky said. "Let's go say hi!"

"Wait, you know them?" I asked.

"I see them at the gym all the time," said Becky, who was a member of the gymnastics team. She marched straight over to them, with me fast on her heels.

"Magic, this is my friend," she said, introducing me by name to him and Jay. The two were quite cordial, which was nice, but really, I had Andy on the brain, and I'd seen another guy that I was interested in, too, so the introductions were short and sweet, and we were on our way. Plus, the dance floor was calling. There, I found my refuge. When the music was playing and my body was moving, nothing else mattered—not grades, not shifty teachers and counselors and white students who treated us like lepers, not guys, not new love or broken hearts, and most certainly not the attention of Earvin Johnson. Music. Movement. That's all I cared about.

By the time the lights came up in the club, I was spent from dancing but felt better than I'd felt in quite some time. I was practically floating out of the venue when I spotted Earvin sitting at a table just beyond where I'd laid my jacket. After collecting my things, I made my way past him toward the exit, but not before tossing him an, "It was nice meeting you."

"Hey, come here," he said, that humongous smile spread across his face.

"What?" I asked as I looked around, to the sides and behind me, sure he was talking to someone else and not me.

"Come here," he repeated. "Why don't you let me get that phone number."

I furrowed my brow and laughed. "What?" I said. "What do you mean?"

"Why you laughing?" he asked.

I turned my body toward him and shrugged. "You haven't spoken to me all night. You didn't dance with me, and now you want my phone number? Are you crazy?"

Besides, we were breaking for Christmas, with three weeks off campus to celebrate the holidays and collect ourselves for the spring semester. I quickly did the math: I give him my phone number, he brags about getting another set of digits to add to what had to be quite the collection, we disappear for break, and he won't remember he so much as met me, much less my name or why he wanted my phone number in the first place. So I told him just that. "You won't even remember my name by the time we come back to campus."

He laughed. "No really, give me the number. I promise you I'll remember. I'll give you a call when we get back to campus."

I narrowed my eyes to size up both him and his promise. Who, I quickly surmised, would it hurt to give the man my number? So I did.

Explaining this to Adrianne was a little tricky; I had, after all, passed along my digits to the man she'd already been calling her husband. When I came clean, she got really quiet but then quickly recovered. "Well, at least one of us got him," she laughed.

Honestly, I didn't think much more of it until I was home one evening with my mom and, while flipping through the TV channels, found the Michigan State versus University of Detroit game. "I should have gone to that game," I said, absentmindedly. And then, when the camera focused on Earvin pushing the ball up court, I pointed him out to my mom: "That's the one I gave my phone number to."

We both laughed and didn't think about it for the rest of the break.

Three weeks later, there I was with Adrianne, back on the campus a few days early so that I could preregister for a few classes I needed but couldn't get into before the semester ended. What do you know? The moment we got the key in the door and pushed it open, the phone rang. Adrianne and I looked at each other, both unsure who knew we were back already.

I picked up the receiver and greeted the caller.

"Hey!" a male voice boomed.

"Hey," I said.

"Is this Cookie?"

"Yes."

"This is Earvin. How are you?"

I looked at Adrianne and mouthed, "It's Magic!" and then leaned back into the receiver.

Earvin continued: "I'm on my way to training table. It's right next door to your dorm, so I was calling to see if you were going to be there and if it would be okay for me to come up and say hi."

"Okay," I said, Adrianne and I still staring at each other in disbelief. "Come on."

To this day, I still don't know how he knew I was back on campus and just walking into my dorm. I hadn't even set down my bags and he was on my phone. And within minutes, he was at our door. Within seconds after that, he, Adrianne, and I were talking and laughing like we'd all grown up together. He came in, he sat down like he lived there, we had a great time, and then he went on to training table.

We were that easy together.

After that, Earvin would come by whenever and hang with us. Some days, we'd talk. Other times, exhausted from a grueling practice, class, and game schedule, he'd crash on my bed. Adrianne and I would be at our desks doing homework, and he'd just climb under my covers and sleep. We barely knew each other, but that was the level of comfort he had with us and we with him.

Soon after, he found out that my birthday was a couple weeks away. "What's the exact date?" he asked one afternoon, folding his lanky body on top of my bedspread.

"January twentieth," I said. "Happy Birthday to me!"

"Okay, I'm going to take you out to dinner on your birthday," he said. "That'll be our first date."

"Like, a real date?" I asked.

"Yeah, a real date," he said easily.

It was a sweet invitation, and I'm not going to lie, I was excited by it. Still, I couldn't bring myself to believe fully that he was serious about dating me. For the life of me, I couldn't imagine why he would pick me. With so many girls on campus throwing themselves at him, I was, frankly, in shock that he even asked me for my number, much less showed any real interest.

My confidence wasn't solidified until a few nights after the invitation, when he offered to accompany me to a dorm party across campus. He picked up Adrianne and me, and we walked in together, only to run smack dab into, of all people, Brent, my old high school sweetheart. Earvin, of course, had no clue whom he was, but Adrianne lost it.

"Cookie! Cookie!" she said, ribbing me.

"What?" I said. I followed her pointed finger to a dark corner of the apartment. Once my eyes focused and registered exactly who I was looking at, I got a little weak in the knees. "Oh my God. What do I do, Adrianne? You know that boy is crazy as hell!"

"Just play it cool," Adrianne said, settling me with a gentle squeeze of my arm. "We're gonna be cool. We're just going to go over here on this side, and he'll stay over there on that side. Act like you don't see him."

I was game for that plan, but I still felt like I needed to say something to Earvin. After all, the moment Brent spotted me, he could very well start trouble, perhaps even pick a fight with my new friend. The last thing I wanted was for this man to be ambushed, especially when we were so new—especially when I didn't even know if he and I were on our way to making ourselves an official couple.

Earvin was neither worried nor daunted by my ex. In fact, ever the competitor, he saw Brent's presence as a direct challenge. "Let him try something," Earvin seethed. He was practically dragging me over to the dark corner where Brent was standing when a slow song started pumping through the speakers. And just when we were standing directly in Brent's line of sight, Earvin pulled me close, our bodies chest-to-chest, hip-to-hip, cheek-to-cheek, slow-dragging to the melody of the song. And ultimately, our hearts.

I was absolutely amused by it all. Brent was not. He said not one word to me the entire night and then, just when we were about to leave, he managed to muster a few words. "I can't believe you're with him," he said angrily.

And just like that, he walked out.

A few days later, I got a three-page letter from Brent insisting that I didn't have what it takes to be the girlfriend of a star. After all, he wrote, "you couldn't even handle me." Adrianne and I laughed at his emotional missive, and then I tossed it into the trash.

After that, I never heard from him again. To this day, I haven't a clue why Brent was on our campus, seeing as he didn't go to school there, presumably didn't know anyone on campus, had to drive almost two hours to get to that party that night, and we hadn't seen or talked to each other in almost six months.

Maybe God put the image of Earvin and me in Brent's mind from the very beginning. Maybe it was fate, too, that led Brent to that party on that night with the specific intent of making him the lightning rod that would bring my intended husband and me closer together. Or maybe it was just God's plan for us. I can't be sure about either, of course. But I do know that on that particular night, Earvin grabbed me by my hand and he never let it go, even when Brent exclaimed his "I can't believe you're with him."

"Let's go get in the car," Earvin said, glaring at Brent. "You're coming with me."

This was the beginning of us.

Chapter Two

Courting Earvin

Maybe I told him I liked the color yellow. I must have. And clearly, Earvin was listening, because he did the sweetest thing any guy who'd ever shown romantic interest in me had done to celebrate my birthday: he showed up to my dorm room grinning, with a dozen yellow roses hidden behind his back.

"What are you doing?" I asked, craning to get a peek.

"Oh, nothing," he said, laughing. "Just stopping by to check out the birthday girl." Earvin playfully shuffled his tall, lean body from side to side to keep me from seeing what he was hiding and then finally pulled the flowers from behind his back in the most dramatic of fashions. "For you," he said, bowing. "Happy Birthday."

Truly, it was an incredibly kind gesture. What guy—a college student, no less—woos a fellow student with roses? But that has always been Earvin's way; even before he entered the NBA, even before he got his big paychecks and all of the spotlight that gave him access to whatever his heart desired, he was extremely thoughtful, incredibly generous, and quite the planner. That's just who he is—a people mover, much like he is as a point guard in a basketball game, telling everybody where the ball is going to go as he pushes it up the court. He cares about not only the event, but also the process of creating it. That part has always tickled me and proved to be one of the charming characteristics that drew me to him. Indeed, his gift giving on my nineteenth birthday didn't stop with the flowers. "Tomorrow," he said, "I'm taking you out. Wear a dress."

To understand how big a deal this was, remember: we were in college. And broker than a joke. Going out for a slice of pizza or a burger at a restaurant that wasn't tied to the campus cafeteria and our lowly meal plans was a rare enough treat. I mean, going to Arby's meant a dude had feelings for you. But Earvin was taking me to an intimate birthday celebration off campus. To a steakhouse. That required we dress up. A *real* restaurant.

The excitement was noticeable, and not just from me. Everyone in my dorm knew the most popular guy on our campus was taking me out, and they were just as anxious as I was about his arrival. Several served as lookouts, standing at the ready to let me know his every movement. By the front door, down the hallway, up the stairs, heads were popping out every few doors with the news: "He's coming through the front door," and "He's walking up the stairs," and "He's headed down the hall—here he comes, Cookie!"

I was anxious when he walked through the door, sure. But boy, his suit broke every bit of nervousness I had. It was that, well, interesting. Swedish knit was "in" back in those days, so he was on point there, but his jacket was reversible: kelly green on one side and plaid on the other. And when he stepped through the threshold of my dorm room, he had that big grin on his face, splashed up against that odd-colored suit. I have to say, my heart skipped a beat; he looked so sweet. "Are you ready?" he asked.

"Yeah," I said, smoothing down my hair and then my little plaid wraparound skirt my mom sent me from her department at J. C. Penney. It came with a matching shawl. It was the only dressy outfit I owned at school.

Somewhere, there is a faded Polaroid picture of the two of us heading out to that date, both of us doing the most with the least, excited about the new. There wasn't a quiet moment—no uneasy silences. Usually, I'm not all that talkative when I'm around people I don't know well—I'm still like this, to this day—but when I was sitting across the table from Earvin, conversation was relaxed. Natural. Full of foolish moments.

"Ya'll come up from Detroit and think you something," he joked. "The big city."

"At least we got nice cars," I ribbed right back. I may or may not have called him a "country bumpkin," too, after making fun of his mode of transportation. See, back home, all the guys had sports cars, like Camaros and Mustangs, Challengers and Grand Prixs, because almost all of them worked in the factory and they made pretty decent money. But at Michigan State, Earvin's car was often the butt of jokes on campus; he drove what we from Detroit referred to as "a Deuce and a Quarter," more formally known as a Buick Electra 225. It was what your daddy drove when he needed a reliable car to cart around his seven kids and a couple nephews, nieces, and play cousins. Earvin would pull that massive boat around the coldest corners of the campus and everybody would start shouting, "Here comes the big, brown Deuce!" Earvin wouldn't pay any of us any mind, because while the brutal Lansing winters made the hottest cars too cold to start, Earvin's old reliable Deuce and a Quarter would roar and roll through subzero temperatures and blizzards like it was a balmy day in July. On the coldest mornings, he would get calls from practically anyone who had his phone number and needed refuge from the bitterly chilly walk across the tundra that was the Michigan State campus. Earvin wasted not one second ribbing anyone who asked. "Oh!" he'd say, laughing. "Everybody wanna get in the big brown Buick now!"

But that's what made Earvin so endearing. No matter the green jacket with the plaid lining, the not-so-cool car, and the superstar status that had the prettiest girls clamoring for his attention, at the base of it all, he was spectacularly regular. What really stole my heart from the very beginning wasn't what Earvin could do for me, but who he was *to* me: a nice, funny, down-home, small-town guy with a big heart from a huge, tight-knit, God-fearing family (he is one of ten children). His parents, to this day, are married. He took pleasure in simple things: hanging out on the swings at the park, hitting up soul food restaurants for meals that reminded us both of home, or sitting in the room at all hours of the day and night, talking and joking about nothing and everything.

Being with him felt . . . easy.

Still, there was a tiny, sinking feeling tucked deep down in my stomach that insisted on twitching while we were at dinner. If it had a voice, it would have totally disrupted our fellow steakhouse diners' conversations with a few loud proclamations: *Magic Johnson is here with me when, clearly, he could have any girl! He's an athlete on campus, and athletes on campus have a certain reputation. Why me? Wait, this steak is expensive. What will he expect me to do for this dinner?*

"Hey, you want to go over to my uncle's house and listen to some music?" Earvin asked as the waitress cleared our plates. "He doesn't live too far from here."

"Okay," I said hesitantly. I looked nervously at my watch. It was close to ten.

If he sensed my nervousness, Earvin sure didn't make it known. But any woman understands the safety concern, if not the outright fear, that comes when you go to a strange place alone with a man you barely know. It gets particularly dicey when the liquor is flowing, the smoke is thick, and the crowd is mostly men who are cursing, and being loud and boisterous. You start considering who knows your whereabouts, what your escape plan would be if he attacked you, what you'd have to do to overpower him and get away, if you have enough money in your purse to call a cab or your mother or a good girlfriend to come get you. And then that little voice started talking again: *Oh my God, what if he does something to me and leaves me on the side of a dark, abandoned road?*

Still, despite my reservations, I got in the front seat of the Deuce and a Quarter and headed over to Earvin's uncle's house. He took my hand gingerly into his and led me into the modest ranch, where an old-school house party was in full effect. The air was thick with the sounds of Marvin Gaye and Parliament, the smoke of Salem and Kool cigarettes, and the jonesing and laughter of a family that was in the middle of a boisterous card game.

"Everybody, this is Cookie," Earvin practically shouted over the din. "Cookie, this is my family."

I smiled and waved, even as I willed my inner punk to trust that Earvin wouldn't let anything happen to me. And soon enough, we were sitting on a sofa in the living room, doing exactly what Earvin said we would be doing: listening to music, sipping on soda (neither of us drank alcohol), and talking. I was sure that Earvin was going to try to jump my bones, but I was wrong: he was such a gentleman. There was no pressure, no expectation. Just pure, genuine interest in me. And as we sat there, listening to Frankie Beverly and Maze, Earvin slowly leaned over and gave me a long, gentle kiss that sent butterflies through my stomach.

Within an hour or so, Earvin finally leaned in close and, to my relief, said the words I'd been waiting to hear: "It's getting late. I should get you back to your dorm. Are you ready to go?"

Earvin slowly leaned over and gave me a long, gentle kiss that sent butterflies through my stomach.

"Sure," I said coolly. My inner voice was much louder, and may have even done a few cheerleader kicks and splits to boot.

We made it through our first date.

· Dating a Superstar ·

Our burgeoning relationship grew as easily as our friendship did. Soon we were showing up to campus parties together regularly, and I was riding shotgun in his car to classes and the dining hall and greeting him and his team with high fives as part of the Spartan Spirits, the squad charged with cheering on the players as they poured onto the court. We hadn't made it official; I wasn't technically his girlfriend. But the way we were carrying on in public, I was sure that's exactly where we were headed.

Still, I wasn't sure I was ready for all that came with the title: the awkward dance toward intimacy; the expectations of a star athlete used to getting what he wanted exactly when he wanted it; the gawking, prying eyes of other women on campus, particularly those with ulterior motives and designs on being seen draped on Earvin's arm. I didn't know how to handle any of it, really, and failed spectacularly when faced with the first challenge: navigating a sexual relationship with a man an enormous amount of women on the campus wanted for themselves.

It happened the night before a big game against the University of Michigan, our school's biggest rival. They had a squad with talent that matched Michigan State's and the local media and our campus were abuzz with anticipation of the match-up. Earvin didn't seem on edge, but he did seek refuge with me in my dorm room. My roommate happened to be out of town that weekend, so we had our space to ourselves, which I'm guessing made it easy for Earvin to think that our easy conversation would naturally progress into kissing and hugging and what comes with that when a man and a woman are in a relationship and alone and ready to share all that it entails. I wasn't with it, though. "Mmmm," I said, gently pushing him away from my lips, my body. "We're not there yet." Earvin reeled back, looking alternately confused and a tad miffed. "You could spend the night," I continued. "But we just can't do anything."

Earvin seemed surprised—disappointed, certainly. The ease of the moments leading up to that very second disappeared, replaced with a heaviness that was palpable. Before I could put the punctuation on my refusal for sex, Earvin was up and heading toward the door. "Oh, okay," he said airily. "I'm gone. I gotta go."

"Wait, you're leaving?" I asked.

"Yeah, I'm out," he said simply.

And just like that, he left.

I thought I'd blown it with him—with us. I was so sure he was mad at me for not having sex with him, and for the next long twenty-four hours, I faced off with the implications of that. After all, one simply did not say no to sex with a man like Earvin, who could be intimate with whomever he chose. What could stop him from leaving my room and my "I'm not ready" proclamation to head over to some other girl's room? What's more: Had I sent him the signal that I was interested in him only as a friend, rather than as a significant other—a boyfriend? Most important, what kind of man was I dealing with if he couldn't understand that I wasn't ready? Who would get dismissive and stomp off like a brat because I stood firm in wanting to get to know him better before I gave myself physically to him? The truth is I was shaken. *Oh my God, he tried it*, I said to myself. I was sure he was mad at me, but I was a tad angry, too.

I didn't see him again until late the next day, after he returned from his basketball game at the University of Michigan. On campus, everybody had attended this huge black fashion show, including me and my roommate, who'd announced the program that night. We were still on a high from that good time when we made our way to the after party. Two of us—my friend, Penny, who was dating a guy on the basketball team, and I—also went with a very specific purpose: to forget our man troubles. I was mad. She was mad. And we were stomping around that campus, looking cute and ticked off and exchanging war stories with all kind of attitude—attitude that was so apparent, Adrianne documented it with her camera for prosperity. I still have that Polaroid shot; in it, my hair, styled prettily in a shoulder-length bob, betrays the smirk smushed across my face. Penny looks mad as hell. Clearly, we were undone. Right after that quick photo shoot, as we were making our way into the party, I spotted Earvin standing outside the dorm, looking casual and nonchalant. I didn't expect to see him there; I thought he'd be tied up with his game. But there he was, dressed to impress, looking like he was on the prowl.

"Hi," I said simply.

"Mmhm," he said. Nothing more. Like I didn't merit more than a grunt.

My heart sank; clearly, he was mad at me. Which only made me madder at him. I tried to go about my business—to act like I wasn't fazed by his cool, dismissive demeanor, but really, I was hurt, and I became only more miffed when I noticed some girl smiling all up in his face and making it painfully obvious that she'd probably be more than happy to do what I wouldn't. Penny was in the same boat with Ron, who also had another woman flitting about.

Much too prideful to stand there and watch, Penny and I went on about our business, trying our best to enjoy the music, the atmosphere, and each other's company, particularly since our men were making a point of doing the same. But staying there, risking humiliation as the guy I liked was acting as if he didn't want to be bothered with me, wasn't an option: I wanted out of that party room. Out of that space. Out of Earvin's rare air. I needed to go back to my dorm room and assess the damage.

In order to leave, though, I had to stroll past Earvin again, a walk I wasn't looking forward to taking, seeing as he'd already dissed me the first time he saw me. Determined to avoid being dismissed again, I quickly decided to walk past like I didn't see him, as casually as I could muster.

"Where you going?" he called out.

I followed his voice and made the mistake of looking into his beautiful eyes. "Uh, to my dorm," I said, trying not to stutter. All that anger, all that worry, all my reservations melted and dripped off me like soft-serve ice cream down a waffle cone on a hot summer day. We'd made a mess out of what should have been a simple conversation about our wants and needs and how we were going to move forward with our relationship, and there he was, seizing the chance to make it right. Despite that I'd relayed to him through my actions that I didn't care, reality was that I did care. I welcomed the airing.

"Come with me," he said, grabbing my hand.

As we made our way out of the building and into the parking lot, out of the corner of my eye, I saw a souped-up red Mustang, standing out like a flash in the dark. I knew that car. I knew the man who drove it. It was my ex-boyfriend, the guy I'd dated after I broke it off with Brent. Our relationship was quick and to the point—so short that I barely counted him as more than a blip on my relationship screen. I'd broken it off with him because it was really clear that we couldn't work—not with him in Detroit acting weird and me in East Lansing, trying to figure out my own self, much less what I wanted in a relationship with a guy who lived hours away. It would have never worked between us, and I made that clear when I told him I wanted to remain strictly platonic friends. He didn't take it well.

"Oh my God, that's Charles," I murmured when I confirmed it was, indeed, my ex. He was sitting on the hood of his car, staring at me, looking a little wild about the eyes. Ready for drama.

"Cookie!" he called out to me.

"No!" I said, shaking my head and holding tight to Earvin's hand. I didn't know why he was there or what he wanted, and I had no intention of finding out. I tried my best to avoid Earvin's gaze, which had read the situation and was full of questions, namely, "Dang, Cookie, you got another crazy man up here on the campus chasing after you?"

While Earvin and I walked across the parking lot, Charles hopped into his car and proceeded to show his whole behind: he revved the engine and made donuts in that bright red Mustang, the sound of the skids outmatched only by the smoke coming off the tires. Earvin simply grabbed my hand a little tighter and led me to his car, ignoring the dramatics.

"We lost tonight," he said quietly, through a nose so stuffed it sounded like he was holding both his nostrils closed. With all of Charles's antics and my ignoring Earvin all evening, I hadn't noticed it, but Earvin was sick and having a hard time breathing.

"Are you okay?" I said, reaching over to touch his forehead. He was warm.

"I'm not feeling so tough," he said.

All of the foolishness we'd been silently arguing about took a backseat to the task at hand: instinctively, I wanted—needed—to help Earvin feel better. He looked so . . . vulnerable. So out of it. I felt sorry for him, and my maternal instinct quickly kicked in.

"You need to take something," I insisted as we walked into his dorm room.

Of course, his medicine cabinet was completely empty; he hadn't so much as an aspirin, let alone nasal decongestant or something to help fight his fever. Rather than go back out, he elected to get into bed.

"You know, last night, I wasn't mad," he said as I pulled the covers up on him and touched his forehead to confirm he'd had a fever. "I really had to go because I needed to get ready for the game. It was a big game and I had to rest."

"Never mind that," I said, both understanding his reaction to my rejection the night before and not caring about it, either. "You need to get some rest so you can fight this cold."

I spent the entire night holding cold compresses to his head, unrolling toilet tissue so that he could blow his nose, and pulling the covers up around his neck so that he could sweat out whatever bug had hit him. Finally, after only a few hours of sleep, I hugged his neck, planted a kiss on his cheek, and went back to my dorm to get ready for my day. Worried about his well-being, I made a point of going to the campus store to pick up some cold medicine to take back to Earvin's room before I headed to class. I didn't bother calling before I made my way over there; I didn't think I needed to.

Wrong.

I tapped on his door gently and got quite a shock when he opened the door; just over his shoulder, I got a glimpse of a girl, in her slippers and robe, standing there like she paid rent. Like that was her place and she was his girl.

"Uh, hello?" I said, my brow furrowed.

"Come on in, Cookie," he said, moving aside and pushing the door wider to let me in.

"Okaaaay," I said, looking at the girl and then back at Earvin, no doubt with a "What the hell is going on here?" look on my face. Trust: just as hard as I was looking at her, she was looking at me.

"Cookie, this is Tony," Earvin said easily. "Tony, Cookie."

And then, we played the waiting game, both of us vying for the one simple answer to the complicated question "who's going to leave first?" I wanted it to be her; I'm sure she wanted it to be me. At the same time, a part of me wanted to preserve my dignity: perhaps I needed to go of my own volition before I got my feelings hurt. In the middle of all that awkward silence—just as I'd decided I was playing myself by sitting there and waiting out this half-dressed woman in Earvin's room—she finally said the words I'd wanted to hear: "I'm gonna see you later. I'm gonna go back to my room."

Earvin walked her to the door and bid her farewell. Before he could get the door completely closed, I was on it: "Well, who was that?" I asked, jabbing my finger in the empty space where she'd stood just seconds earlier.

"Oh, that's my friend from high school," Earvin said easily.

"An old friend?" I asked. "Just a friend?"

"Well, we dated in high school, but that was a long time ago. There's nothing going on; she lives here in the dorm, and she stopped by to say hello. That's it," Earvin insisted.

"Okay, whatever," I said, not really buying what he was selling. "Here's some medicine. I hope you're feeling better soon."

I pushed past him, down the steps, and out the front door of his dormitory, confused and mad and, worst of all, unsure about what had just transpired. Right there, in my face, was all that I'd feared about a relationship with someone like Earvin—someone who was popular and successful and on his way to a rarefied air that would afford him unfettered admiration from the opposite sex. He was special, I knew that. In almost three months of dating, we'd connected—of that, I was sure. But there was an unknown variable there: though we'd grown to be great friends, and everyone on campus recognized that we were a "thing," I hadn't gotten the official title from Earvin, and, if I were totally honest with myself, there was absolutely nothing to keep him from choosing to be a player rather than being faithful and committed solely to me. I was getting a taste of all that being a mate of someone of his stature would require; our college campus was a literal petri dish of what, surely, I'd face if we managed to become a couple, make it out of Michigan State, and live a life together, with him a superstar and me that superstar's wife. How many more girls would I find in his room, sitting there, comfortable as they please in their pajamas and robe and slippers, like they were planning to stay for a while or, worse, had already had their fun?

This time, I wasn't about to let the uncomfortable silence between us be the beginning and ending of the conversation on where we stood. After a day or so to think about it, I made my way back to his dorm and asked for some clarification and a more definitive explanation on just what I meant to him—on just where he saw our relationship going. I wanted to know, too, if Tony was someone I needed to worry about.

"Who is she?"

"She's just a friend of mine," he said matter-of-factly. Easily. His demeanor never once rose to the level of alarm in my head. "Really, it was just a coincidence that she stopped by right when you got here. She lives in the dorm, that's why she was in her robe and slippers. Nothing more."

I didn't want to dismiss what the entire scenario looked like, but he had a point about her style of dress. Plus, the truth was I'd spent practically the entire night with him save for a few hours, and was back early the next morning, leaving very little time for her to bring over her clothes, sleep with him, rest, and then get dressed up in her robe and slippers just in time for my early-morning medicine run. I had to reconcile in my mind what to believe—to trust that he was going to make the right decision when women threw themselves at him and especially when it came time for him to tell me the truth, even if that truth was devastating. I decided that he'd given me explanation enough and that focusing on her was taking away from our focus on us.

"Tell me this," I said, finally. "Are we together or not?"

He hesitated and let out a little laugh; my heart sank, if only a little bit.

"Yeah," he said. "Not completely, though."

His face betrayed my frown. "No, no, you're my girl!" he said. "I'm just playing. You're my girl."

And from there on out, when he introduced me to his friends, his teammates, his family, and his acquaintances, that was my title: "This," he would say, "is Cookie, my girl."

· Chapter Three ·

An Uneasy Alliance

Finally, it was official: I was Earvin's girlfriend. But there was still an unease that came with the title. I knew there were women vying for his attention. I was clear that, if the opportunity presented itself, they wouldn't hesitate to try to take my place. That always was bubbling just below the surface. Still, I was clear-eyed on the mission: if I were to be in a committed relationship with Earvin, I'd have to trust him. And if I were to do what was best for me, I'd have to focus on my studies and fulfilling my own passion rather than expending all my energy chasing down rumors of infidelity.

There were times that I questioned his commitment, though, particularly when he insisted I stop waiting for him outside the locker room after his games. "You go straight to your room, and

I'll be there as soon as I get done," he'd say. Most of the time, that's what he did: he would come by, pick me up, and we'd go get something to eat or go back to his apartment and hang out. Soon enough, though, I had some questions—questions that had me wondering why, exactly, I couldn't wait for him after the games like his family and all the other players' girlfriends did. In fact, we actually had a huge argument about it, with him warning me to stay away. "But who was that girl who leaped into your face when you came out the locker room?" I questioned.

"Cookie, I don't even know who you're talking about," he insisted. "People always come see me after the games. She could have been a cousin. She could have been a fan. I don't have any control over that."

"But you don't have a problem when these girls show up, either," I said, accusatorially.

"You know what? You don't have to wait after the games for me," he huffed.

That was his final word. But I didn't listen. I needed to see what was going on outside that locker room, no matter his insistence that I stay away.

So on this one particular game night, I showed up to the waiting area with my friend Penny, whose boyfriend played on the team, too. I spent the entire time trying to take stock of just who was there to meet whom—if the girl in the corner was a cousin from Lansing or a Magic Johnson fan from campus. "Who is that over there?" I'd ask no one in particular, squinting my eyes and cocking my head to the side.

I did see Earvin's parents and, sure enough, when he came out of the locker room, he went straight to them. Just beyond their heads, he saw me, standing there, waiting. Our eyes locked. I smiled; he glared and turned his gaze back to his parents. Soon enough, he led them over to some chairs, sat down, and talked to them for what seemed like an eternity, then he chatted up another person and another person still, while I sat there, waiting for him—at the very least—to acknowledge my presence, but hoping he'd come over and take my hand. I was perplexed. So was Penny. Her boyfriend, Ron, was simply confused.

"Why are we just standing here?" he asked, looking at his watch and surveying the emptying room.

"Penny can't leave because I want her to wait with me until Earvin and I connect," I said, my eyes still on my boyfriend.

Sure enough, Earvin made Penny, Ron, and me wait there until there was no one else in that stadium but the janitors. Then he sauntered our way.

"Hey, Penny," he said, waving. Then he turned to Ron. "See you at practice tomorrow. I'm out."

He said not one word to me. Instead, he turned on his heels and walked right out the door.

"Wait," I said, calling after him, but he just kept walking.

Shocked that he would be so incredibly rude to me, but too prideful to ask him what in the world he was doing, I just let him walk on.

I didn't hear from him until the next day. He called and before I could finish saying "Hello," he was on my case: "Did you learn your lesson?"

I was quiet.

"I told you I had to talk to a bunch of people afterward, and there's no need for you to be standing around waiting through that," he continued. "I want to see you after the games. But I want to come to you."

This was Earvin's way. I had to trust not only that he wasn't hiding anything from me, but also that he had my best interests at heart. This turned out to be a simple proposition—a precursor, for sure, to how we would manage our relationship in public once he got to the NBA. He needed me to understand that I could be secure in our relationship and my standing in it without being attached to his hip. But, most important, he needed me to know that he was counting on me for something much more grand: the critical support and home base star athletes need to keep them grounded and assured that, beyond the glamour, beyond the accolades, beyond the users

> *This turned out to be a simple proposition—a precursor, for sure, to how we would manage our relationship in public once he got to the NBA.*

and shysters on the take, someone loves them unconditionally, has their back, and can give them solitude. Rest.

Earvin and I walked a long, winding road to get to where he fully trusted me to be that person for him. A large part of why it was such a long journey had to do with fear—his. Earvin simply did not want to be put in a box, to feel like he was being tied down before he was ready. This became painfully evident early in our relationship, during our sophomore year. We were in good standing with each other, spending as much time together as possible, given the amount of traveling Earvin had to do as a member of our school's special teams in the summer and both of our hectic school schedules in our second year at Michigan State. When we were together, it was all love and good times—if he wasn't in my dorm room, I was at his apartment. On rowdier occasions, we went to parties together, but mostly, we'd keep to ourselves, low-key and quiet, getting to know each other over lunch or hugging, giggling, and sharing ourselves on the swings at a special park we'd disappear to together. We had fun; it was nice. Us.

But then came a day when Earvin had been zipped away to New York to do a *Sports Illustrated* cover, one that would turn into the iconic image of him dunking a basketball in a top hat, tuxedo tails, and dress shoes, with that wide smile as bright as the cover line: "Super Sophs: Michigan State's Classy Earvin Johnson." He was really excited about it—as he should have been: I mean, a *Sports Illustrated* cover!—and after he finished up the photo shoot and interview, he called me at my dorm to recap his good fortune. I was so happy for him and happy, too, that after all the excitement, he made a point of sharing it with me. I hung up the phone swooning, relaying the good news to my roommate, Adrianne, and a guy she'd been dating, an old friend of Earvin's, from Lansing. I thought nothing more of it—just went on back to the business of entertaining my friends, doing my schoolwork, and looking forward to seeing Earvin again.

Well, for the latter, I waited quite a long time. When Earvin got back from New York, he didn't bother calling me. Not once, for weeks, and I had absolutely no clue why. Finally, I started dialing his number and leaving messages for him: "What's going on? Where are you?"

He would never call back. And then another week passed without him calling, or stopping by, or giving me anything more than a cursory "What's up?" when we did run into each other on campus. Before I knew it, an entire month zoomed by with me worried and thinking, *Well, I don't understand. What did I do? What did I say?* Then, finally, I caught up to him.

He was cold—distant. I was straightforward. "What's going on with you?" I asked. "Why did you stop calling me?"

Earvin was quiet—pensive. Finally, he answered. "You know, sometimes people start thinking that they can control other people, and they start thinking that they have access to them."

Confused, I furrowed my brow. "What are you talking about?"

"Nothing," he said, quickly winding up our conversation and leaving me standing there, bewildered.

I came to find out much later that Earvin's friend, the one who'd been dating my best friend, teased Earvin about calling me from New York. "This girl got your nose wide open, huh?" he told Earvin. "You calling her from New York like you're checking in with your wife, and she's in the room making it seem like, 'Oh, I got him!'"

Truly, that was the last thing Earvin needed to hear from his male friends, some of whom, I'm sure, were quite invested in their friend keeping his "options" open as he readied himself for the fast, glamorous life of a professional basketball star. He did not want to be controlled, and he certainly didn't want anyone—not his friends, not me—to think that he could and would bend at my will. So he backed off.

Many more weeks would go by before we ran into each other again, and he agreed to sit and talk awhile, only to reiterate that I didn't "control" him. I made it my mission to make him understand that controlling him was not something I was interested in. "I'm not that kind of person," I insisted. "I'm not one of those bossy girlfriends making scenes and bringing drama."

But rather than say it, I needed to prove it. I learned during our time dating back then that space is what he craved—the ability to feel free but, at the same time, know that I was there. This translated into things like the two of us going to parties together, then separating and dancing with other people and, occasionally, with each other, then leaving together. As long as we left as a couple, both of us were cool.

But that uneasy truce lasted only a short while. A few weeks later, when I got into his car, I spotted a series of photographs on the floor; in them, a fellow student was dressed in a gown with a fur coat, posed with Earvin, who was sporting a tux and that trademark grin.

This time, I was the angry one. "What is this?" I asked, shoving the pictures into Earvin's face. The venue looked familiar: it was the Delta Ball, a popular, exclusive soiree for the sorority Delta Sigma Theta. "Wait: Did you take this girl to the Delta Ball?" I asked.

"Yeah, well, I kinda had to," he said casually, then quickly added: "She's just a friend."

I'm pretty sure the steam coming off my head fogged up his car windows. We'd been back together for only a few weeks, and I'd agreed, under no uncertain terms, to make sure I gave him his space, and here he was, repaying the favor by going out on exclusive dates with our classmates. Noticing my ire, Earvin tried to do more damage control. "Cookie, I said she's just a friend. I was doing her a favor."

"No, you don't do favors like that," I said. "We're supposed to be together. You taking her to the ball is a big deal."

Let's just say the drive back to the dorm was every bit as heated as that steam pouring out of my ears. I was willing to give him space, of course, if that was what he needed. But my require-ments were very simple: if we were going to be in a committed relationship, it couldn't be a one-way deal, with me giving my all and receiving not even the most basic of requirements from my man. I was—and remain so today—a simple woman with an easy, straightforward demeanor, who required little more than respect and a pledge of exclusivity from the man I loved. And, in my mind, Earvin had displayed that he wasn't ready to give me either. That was a deal breaker for me. It was difficult knowing that there were women from Michigan to Massachusetts, Los Angeles to New York City, and every other locale in between, vying for Earvin's attention, but I got through it because I willfully believed him when he said it was just him and me. When you sign up for that kind of love in the glare of the spotlight, you must be prepared to have a certain level of trust, not just in your significant other, but your instincts. I made the conscious decision to trust Earvin, not just for the sake of our relationship, but also for my sanity. Otherwise, I would have driven myself crazy worrying about who was trying to get his attention, who was telling lies to break us up, and whom he may have been interested in other than me. But here was evidence, splayed across a series of Polaroid shots, that he had no intention of giving me what I needed to make our relationship work. I was devastated. And livid.

When he pulled up in front of my dorm, I turned to him and made it plain: "You know, Earvin, you're going to have to make a decision between her and me. You can't say we're together and take other women out on dates. Are you dating her?"

"I don't have to answer that," he sniffed.

"Oh, really?" I said, the pitch of my voice raised several octaves. "So I'm going to ask you again: Are you dating her? Because I thought we were together."

"Listen, Cookie, you can't control me or tell me what to do."

"Well, I know this much," I said. "You can't date both of us. So either you're dating me or you're dating her. Which is it?"

"I don't have to answer that question," he insisted.

"Well, then, I'll answer it," I screamed. "You're not dating both of us. I'm out."

"Fine!" Earvin yelled back as I snatched open the car door and climbed out. "Go!"

As it would turn out, Earvin was dating the girl in the picture. She was the niece of a faculty member and mentor who had ingratiated himself to Earvin with the hopes that he could be his agent and help ease Earvin through his transition from college basketball to the pros. He was like a father figure to Earvin, and his niece, a beautiful, smart pre-med student who was president of the sorority and from a well-to-do family that sent her to Michigan State in a sports car, was, in that mentor's eyes, the kind of woman someone of Earvin's stature needed on his arm. I'd compounded the situation by giving Earvin that "her or me" ultimatum. Rather than simply say, "No, I'm not really dating her, I'm with you," he assumed I was doing the one thing he couldn't stand: exercising my control over him. So he left me and went to her. I was devastated.

This would be the first of many times in our romance journey that Earvin's fear of commitment and penchant for alpha male dominance would tear us apart. Truly, it was an act of sheer will, a deep, unyielding love and a commitment to laying our fears aside for the greater good of commitment that brought us back together.

· Break Up to Make Up, That's All We Do ·

A few months into our sophomore year, after we broke up, the love of my life had added a long list of on-court accomplishments to his bustling basketball résumé: a Big 10 Championship trophy and a Michigan State NCAA win over Indiana University set him up lovely for a chance as a first-round draft pick into the NBA, and everyone was excited about the prospects.

I was simply crushed.

Despite the fact that Earvin and I had exchanged phone calls a few times after we broke up, leaving open the door to a possible reunion, things had apparently become serious between Earvin and the sorority girl. I found out just how much the toughest way possible: via a press conference during the Michigan State NCAA championship win banquet. Earvin stood in front of the cameras and thanked his date for "looking beautiful" and "being there" and "helping" him through the long, tough road to the finals.

"Oh my God!" I said, shaking my head at the television screen as the words tumbled from his lips. It hurt to see him give public credit to and acknowledge her, something he'd never done with me; it meant that I had officially been replaced. He was no longer thinking about me.

Done with the entire affair, I set to the business of focusing on me. My mission was to soar through my sophomore and junior years and graduate the following year, with at least one internship under my belt and a job waiting for me on the other side. Settling down with a man was no longer a part of my agenda; I decided I would simply date, and that's exactly what I did.

Still, though he had clearly moved on, Earvin wouldn't let me be. Somehow, he found out I'd been out with a guy from Lansing, his hometown, and that merited a phone call. "You dating Chuckie now?" he asked one evening when he called me unexpectedly in my dorm.

"Shut up and get out of my life," I said, giggling but only half joking.

Earvin had it all wrong. The truth was I'd gone out on only one date with Chuckie, but whatever that was never got off the ground; I didn't want to be bothered with him. Still, Earvin didn't need to know that. All bets between Earvin and me were officially off, though, when he was drafted into the NBA by the Los Angeles Lakers, and sorority girl followed him there, securing a spot in a prestigious medical school in the same city.

Earvin was officially gone.

I swore off dating basketball players after that, but my ban didn't last long; Kevin, a University of Detroit recruit who was quickly making a name for himself on the Michigan State team after Earvin left for LA, made it known that he was interested.

"Nope," I said quickly, without even thinking twice about it, when he asked me out the first time, and the second time and third time, too. "I don't want any more parts of the basketball crazy," I added. I was a junior by then, fully focused on graduating and moving on with my life. "I'm just trying to get out of here, and I'd like to do that with as little drama as possible."

But Kevin wouldn't hear of it. For a year, he kept pressing the issue, trying his best to get me to date him. Finally, on the evening of my birthday in my senior year, Kevin broke me down: he caught me in a celebratory mood at the same club where I'd met Earvin, turned on the charm, and convinced me to go out with him for one date. That date turned into a full-fledged romance that allowed me finally to feel like I'd let down my guard—like it was okay to move on.

Until one fateful spring afternoon when Earvin, home early after the Lakers lost the chance to qualify for the championship series, showed up to campus. I wasn't expecting him, but as Kevin was walking me back to my dorm room, there he was: Earvin in his big, pretty, blue Mercedes-Benz, cruising to a stop at the stop sign. When we each got a look at one another, Kevin, Earvin, and I froze. Not a word was exchanged, not a movement was made. It was as if the birds stopped chirping and the earth stopped its rotational axis.

Finally, Earvin waved. He gave that smile and a flick of his wrist and then sat there in his pretty car, watching my new boyfriend and me cross the street. Then, he went his way and we went ours.

"So, how do you feel about that?" Kevin asked.

"How do I feel about what?" I asked.

"That—him seeing us together," he said.

I was quiet for a moment. "We're not together," I said. "It doesn't matter."

It was Kevin's turn to get quiet, talking again only as we approached the front door to my dormitory. He pulled me close. "I want you to come to the pick-up game tomorrow," he said.

"Really?" I asked. "Why?" Kevin had never asked me to go to a pick-up game before, and I wasn't quite sure what had changed between us to warrant an invitation.

"You know, I'd just like you to be there and watch me play for a little bit," he said, shrugging. "It'll be nice to have you there."

Though I thought the invitation strange, I was certainly pleased. It was nice to be wanted—to be acknowledged publicly by my boyfriend in a space that was important to him, among people who meant something to him. It was certainly a welcome change from being barred from postgame interaction with Earvin just a couple years earlier. I thought the gesture was sweet.

Really, it was a disaster.

When Kevin and I arrived to the gym, Earvin was there, waiting to play in a pick-up game, as he was wont to do when he was in town and bored and itching to do what he loved. Though he appeared laid-back, he had this gleam in his eyes—a gleam that I knew translated into one thing: trouble. Poor Kevin, so completely and thoroughly unaware of what was about to go down, tossed a glance at Earvin, then squared his shoulders and strutted to the court.

The games began. Earvin and Kevin played against each other in a generally genial match. No one got hurt. But I was still breathing uneasy, knowing Earvin was up to something. Sure enough, he racked up a set of back-to-back fouls that got him tossed out of the game, then headed straight to the seat next to where I was sitting, that wide grin spread across his face.

"Hey, what's going on?" he said casually. "How you been? You looking real good."

"Thank you," I stammered, half looking at him, half looking at Kevin, who was glaring from the court.

Soon enough, the pick-up game Kevin was playing in ended, and another began; Earvin joined in, my ex-boyfriend squaring up against my new partner.

It was ugly.

Earvin showed absolutely no mercy to Kevin; he took him to school, pulling out every last trick and all manner of NBA moves to humiliate my new boyfriend. Earvin shut him down so horribly, so thoroughly, the entire gym erupted into a collection of winces and squeals and "Oh, damn!" proclamations. I fought myself not to bury my face in my hands. *What did you walk into and why didn't you see this coming?* was all I could muster in a conversation with myself as I nervously waited for the nightmare to end. When, finally, it was over, Earvin put the final nail in Kevin's coffin: with everyone in the gym watching him, he clapped his hands, dramatically and loudly dusted them off, and then walked over to where I was sitting. "Good seeing you," he said, smiling, before strolling away.

It goes without saying that the walk back to my apartment was intense, quiet. I could count the number of words exchanged between Kevin and me on two hands: "Is everything okay? You all right?" I asked.

"Yeah, I'm good," he mumbled without looking at me.

"Okay," I said as we walked onto the sidewalk separating our apartments.

Not another word was said: Kevin went his way, I went mine.

Ten minutes later, as I was getting out my books to study and considering ways to make it up to Kevin, there was a knock at the door. I opened it, ready to gush and declare my extreme "like" to Kevin, with the intent of making him feel a little better about what had happened in the gym. But it wasn't Kevin. It was Earvin.

He didn't bother saying hello; he just walked in and started running his mouth: "I just came by to say hi," he said as he strolled into my room. "I haven't seen you in so long and all of a sudden, there you are in the street with that guy."

"What's it to you?" I asked, annoyed. Honestly, I was a tad disgusted with Earvin's behavior; though we'd talked occasionally, I hadn't seen him in person in almost two years. I didn't take too kindly to his showing up, uninvited, into my personal space and launching the equivalent of a Molotov cocktail into the middle of my burgeoning relationship. After all, he'd had no problem moving on; his sorority girl was in California with him, living what was supposed to be my life. I deserved to be happy, too—to find a love of my own—and my ex had no right to stymie that. "Why do you even care about what I'm doing? Shouldn't you be focused on your little friend who followed you out to California?"

"She didn't come to be with me," he insisted.

"You still playing that card?" I asked. "Whatever, Earvin."

And then, just as easily as we argued, we fell into that easy groove—talking about nothing and everything, joking and laughing and making fun. It was just like old times between two old friends, and before I knew it, we'd both let our guards down and started remembering what we'd had together.

It felt right.

Soon, our talk turned into playful wrestling, the kind of tussling lovers do when one thing is about to lead to another and lovers do what lovers do. I was laying on my back on the floor, and Earvin was hovering over me and we were giggling and our bodies were intertwined and slowly, surely, he leaned his face into mine, and I closed my eyes, ready to feel his lips against my lips. Earvin took his time; the anticipation was torturous. I waited. And waited. And waited, with my lips primed and ready.

But, nothing.

I opened my eyes to find Earvin looking down at me, smirking.

"Yeah," he laughed. "I want you to know what you're missing. Get rid of that guy and then we can talk."

My husband has always had a flair for the dramatic, and this was no exception.

Kevin seemingly dropped off the face of the planet, never once calling me, stopping by, or talking to me again after that brutal basketball game meeting with Earvin. He literally disappeared. As did Earvin. We talked a few times, sure, while I tried to move on with my life—through a summer internship, through more school, through graduation, through my exhaustive job search after college and my landing of a job in fashion merchandising in Toledo, Ohio. But he was living his own, separate life. And I was busy trying to collect one of my own.

Little did I know, though, that each of these things was simply a move in the long, slow dance between the NBA superstar and the quiet ex-girlfriend—a dance that would eventually lead to our forever.

· Chapter Four ·

The Runaway Groom

It was Earvin I wanted—the man who, whenever he had so much as a three-day break from playing basketball, rushed back to Lansing to be with his family; who liked playing card games, listening to music, and throwing barbecues with his childhood friends; who found the simplest, most beautiful pleasure going to the park, just the two of us, and talking and laughing and pushing me on the swing. That guy—he was the one I knew, the one I loved, the one I envisioned being by my side as I pursued my long-held passion to have a successful career in fashion. I wanted no part of Magic; I preferred a simpler life. Reality. And my reality was this: Earvin was off being Magic and didn't want to commit to the quiet girl from back home, and I was fully focused on becoming a clothing buyer and living a quiet life outside of the spotlight—most certainly outside of Magic Johnson's shadow.

At first, even this wasn't a simple proposition. I was heartbroken over breaking up with Earvin, and my fledgling relationship with Kevin was over. I was back home after graduating from college and failing miserably at finding a gig, while all my college friends were too busy starting their careers—indeed, their lives—to really connect the way we had at Michigan State. So my transition after leaving school was a tricky, sticky one. I didn't mind living with my mother and brother again, but it bothered me greatly that I couldn't support myself and had no job prospects. I was a Mary Kay rep for a while and made a little money, but definitely not enough to earn one of those signature pink Cadillacs, considering I didn't know many people in Detroit to sell makeup to outside of a few of my mother's friends. I appreciated the sales skills I picked up, but what I really wanted to do was to work full-time, and the longer my job search stretched, the more depressed I got.

Even Earvin, who'd taken to calling me occasionally and trying to wind his way back into my good graces, recognized how depressed I was about the situation and, out of the kindness of his heart, offered a helping hand. "Why don't you move out here to LA with me?" he suggested during one of our phone conversations. "I'll take care of you."

Now, I fully understand that most would have quickly kissed good-bye everyone they ever knew and loved, packed up all their belongings, closed their eyes, and jumped feet first into the pool of bright, glamorous Hollywood lights that Magic Johnson swam in, but that's the exact opposite of what I wanted. I couldn't trust that by following behind him I wouldn't lose myself and the things I held dear. What's more, I didn't want to put myself into the position of depending on this man and driving myself crazy worrying about what he was doing and with whom. Surely, I would have had a nervous breakdown. We were friends. I had no claims to him, no sway over him. Easily, it could have gotten ugly. "That's sweet," I told him that day when he made the offer. "But I'm going to pass on that. I have to find my own way."

Finally, I did. I got an entry-level position at Alliance Department Stores, a Toledo, Ohio-based company that was a part of the Mercantile Corporation, which owned several groups of department stores spread across several states. I started out as an assistant to the manager of a jewelry department, the ground floor of a six-year program to become a buyer. I loved the job and especially appreciated being able to start living my own life, on my own terms.

In the meantime, slowly but surely, over the course of my first year in Toledo, Earvin started winding his way back into my heart and I into his. The phone calls became more frequent, the conversations longer and more in-depth. Finally, he found his way to Toledo one weekend while home in Michigan recovering from knee surgery, and before I knew it, we were in the middle of a relationship again.

Earvin always treated me like a queen; a bona fide lover of fashion, he adored buying me clothes, shoes, and jewelry and seeing me dressed up head-to-toe in what he'd purchased. He'd be so proud taking me out with the other players and their wives when there were special celebrations. I was always his plus one to private affairs they attended together, like Kareem Abdul-Jabbar's birthday party, baby showers, and team family outings and the like. The first time I got a whiff of his celebrity was when he took me to see *The Wiz*, starring Stephanie Mills. It was the first Broadway play I'd ever been to, and there we were, sitting right up front, basking in the light of that amazing production. Sitting right in front of us was the comedian and actor T. K. Carter, who turned around and held a friendly conversation with us, as if we were old friends. I remember thinking, *Wow, that guy is a celebrity!* That part, in the beginning, was interesting. A little starry.

But it was the quieter moments—not the glitz and glamour, not the acceptance of those who were inhabiting Earvin's life—that put us back on the road to love. Nothing made us happier than to wake up in each other's arms and then lie around his apartment, watching our favorite movies, having good conversation over a great meal. He would go to practice in the mornings and come back to his place with a simple egg and bacon sandwich for me, or, if practices were in the evening, he'd bring back a Fat Burger fixed just the way I liked it. Those things, more than meeting any celebrity, more than hanging out with any of his teammates and their families, made me happiest. We did simple things that built on our connection to each other.

And then I would say good-bye to that fantasyland in Los Angeles and head back to Toledo, where I was building my own life, my own self. Deep down, I knew I wasn't that woman who was comfortable riding shotgun in his fancy car and holding his hand as we pushed through the crowds and paparazzi and past the velvet ropes. Truth is I knew he wasn't comfortable with that lifestyle, either. The façade was there, sure, but deep down, Earvin was still that guy who found refuge—home—with me. And I think my resistance to that lifestyle and my insistence on finding my own way, in my own time, in my own space, made him *see* me. Made him want me.

I had some angels on my side working on him, too. Lakers coach Pat Riley's wife, Chris, was a strong advocate. One night out at dinner, while Earvin was off chatting with the coach, she grabbed my hands in hers and pulled me close to her. "Cookie, I've been telling Magic forever that I want to meet you! I've been asking him, 'Where is your girl?' I really worry about him, you know. He needs a home life. He needs somebody to take care of him. I ask him where you are and he says, 'My girl lives in Toledo,' and then I say, well, why is she there?"

She talked a mile a minute, leaving very little room for me to get in a word edgewise. But I hung on to those words because she was confirming what I knew: Earvin needed a home. He needed somebody who really cared about him. He needed me—not just when he was riding high, but especially when he was feeling low. When he lost a game or he was hurt or he was facing off against challenges from fellow players, he needed that grounding, the person who could remind him that it was going to be all right. I'd come to find out later that the most important people in Earvin's life were telling him the same things—not just in word but also in deed. His then-best friend, Isaiah Washington, had married his longtime girl-friend just a year before, and he was always in Earvin's ear about the importance of building a home and a family and opening his heart to "the one" who would be loyal, honest, and willing to walk by his side during the ups and downs of life's journey. That positive reinforcement from the people who surrounded him solidified my standing; I was assured not just by them but by the one who counted most—Earvin. There were never any incidents in which I was confronted by any women from his past. His intentions for me were pure, and because we were in a long-distance relationship, I chose to trust that—to trust him.

On one particular trip to visit his family for a summertime gathering in Lansing, I was rocked with some unexpected news. I'd happily lost myself in conversation with his sisters and mother while Earvin took off, presumably to run an errand, only to arrive back to the house with a guest: a little boy, about age three, wide-eyed and clinging to his hand. When the two entered the kitchen, everybody stopped talking, but their eyes, darting from Earvin to the toddler to one another, told the story: the little boy was someone important. Someone who had the potential to change things—the power to change the air. And boy, did he.

"Cookie," Earvin said after what seemed an eternity of awkward silence. "This is Andre. Andre is my son."

"What?" I asked, confused about whether I'd heard him correctly.

Just then, poor little Andre, no doubt scared to death, burst into tears as he searched for a familiar face. There was none to be found; Andre, as it turned out, was meeting not just me but Earvin's entire family for the first time.

"Calm down," Earvin told the little boy in his no-nonsense way as he hoisted him into his arms. "It's going to be okay."

And with that, Earvin handed the child to his mother, and disappeared again, this time with his brother. Another round of silence and darting eyes abound before one of his sisters explained that Earvin had only recently found out Andre was, indeed, his son, a product of a sexual relationship with a friend of the family while the two of us were broken up. His mother explained that she'd thought it important that Earvin take responsibility for Andre and include him in his life.

I didn't know what to say—how to respond. I had to process the shock of it all before I could even begin to understand the details.

By the time Earvin's mom settled the little boy down, fed him, and helped him get comfortable around all of us, Earvin arrived back to the house and called me aside to explain. "She's my sister's best friend," he began. He was straightforward but contrite. "We had a one-time fling years ago, but she ended up pregnant." For years, he added, Andre's mother insisted Earvin was the father, but he didn't believe her until a DNA test proved otherwise. "This is the first time I've taken him from the house by myself."

Shocked as I was by the news, I embraced Andre because he was a part of Earvin. I trusted my then-boyfriend when he divulged the details of his dalliance with Andre's mother, and took pride in the fact that he was embracing his role as a father—a role that gave me a peek at the kind of parent he would be to the children I hoped one day we would have together. Our ability to move forward was testament to the fact that what we had was real: I loved Earvin and he loved me. A year into our dance, he made his intentions clear: Earvin asked me to marry him.

His proposal was romantic but really informal. He was home for the summer in Michigan and just about to make his way back to Los Angeles when he stopped by his agent's house and asked me to meet him there. We had dinner and sat around talking about everything and nothing, and then, just as I was preparing to leave, Earvin pulled me into a room. "Cookie," he said, "I love you. I want to marry you. Will you marry me?"

I knew he loved me, he certainly knew I wanted to be married, and I was happy that he'd asked because I loved him, so

I quickly said, "Yes." It was so awkward, though, and Earvin was nervous as all get out. And just as quickly as he asked, the moment was over. There was no celebration. We didn't call anyone over to toast. An hour later, I was driving to Toledo, and he was heading back to Los Angeles. I didn't realize it then, but thinking back on it, I should have known what was coming next.

· *Breaking My Heart* ·

The way he called off the wedding was sudden, quick, and cold: "I can't do it," he told me in a hasty, unexpected phone call. I was blindsided: I'd taken the lead in dealing with the minutiae of the wedding planning—What font on the invitations? Would we have a band or a deejay at the reception? Would the bridesmaids wear sweetheart necklines or strapless?—and trusted that he was fully invested in giving his input, even if he did so with a bit of indifference. I would tell him about another choice I made, and he would say, "Okay," and quickly change the subject, but I thought nothing of this. He was busy; the wedding planning was my job, and I was happy to do it.

Which is why I didn't see the breakup coming. We'd just hung up the phone after discussing the church I'd chosen for us to exchange our nuptials when Earvin called back. "Listen, we have to talk," he said, gloom rimming his words.

My heart pounded. I could tell from the way he dragged his words, from the somber, dark silence between each of them, that something was terribly wrong.

"I can't do it," he continued. "I cannot do it."

"Do what?" I asked.

"I can't get married."

"You can't get married?" I echoed back, wanting to make sure I heard him correctly.

"I can't do it," he said.

Now, I didn't know it at the time, but I would find out much later that Earvin was going through some things. This was right around the time that he was suffering from a bout of shingles and had gotten really stressed out about not being on the court. Off court, he was fighting some personal battles over finances and trying hard to protect himself and his fortune. When I finally did find out about all of this, his breaking up with me made a little more sense; he was under an incredible amount of pressure. But in real time, before I knew of his struggles and the stress they were causing, all I knew was that this man, whom, after our last breakup, I'd been dating and loving and serious about for almost four years, didn't want to marry me. The only reasonable explanation I could think of at that precise moment, without all the information I needed, was that there must be someone else. He loves her, not me.

"Who is she? Do you love her?" I asked, reaching for an explanation.

Earvin assured me, though, that there was no one. "I just can't, that's all."

"How is this happening over the phone? We can't break up over the phone," I insisted.

I could barely put the phone back in its cradle; I was absolutely devastated. My hands trembled as I looked down at my engagement ring, glistening in the glow of the light on my nightstand. I lay down in my bed and sobbed into my pillow until, finally, sleep put me out of my misery for the evening.

The next few weeks were a flurry of girlfriend pow-wows, long talks with my mother and sister and Earvin's sisters, too, and some serious soul-searching of my own. Taking into account the thoughts of those I trusted, plus my relationship history with Earvin and a heaping dose of common sense thrown in for good measure, I came to the only logical conclusion I could muster for why the love of my life didn't want to marry me: I simply didn't fit into his plans. No matter how hard he tried to embrace it, that level of commitment was frightening to Earvin, every bit as much at that moment as it was when we were in college and he was railing against being tied down by a girlfriend who he thought was trying to direct his life. Back at Michigan State, he was popular with the potential to be a star, but now, he was bona fide: he'd had several NBA championships under his belt, he'd been living on his own in Los Angeles the way he saw fit and, at age twenty-six, he had his routines and rules that, undoubtedly, would have had to change in order to accommodate a wife. No matter how much encouragement he was getting from his friends, no matter that his parents, who were still married, set the example for the importance and sanctity of marriage, no matter that he loved me and I loved him and we were good together, at that moment in time, Earvin just couldn't see how to fit me into his life, and he wasn't ready to try.

I needed him to say that to me in person, though—to look me in the eyes and tell me that he did not want to be with me. A quick, terse phone call wasn't going to cut it for me. I insisted on an in-person conversation, and he agreed to meet me at his hotel when the Lakers were in town to play the Detroit Pistons.

I was a bundle of nerves when I knocked on his door; I knew that what I said in that moment could change the course of both of our lives—make my fiancé understand, truly, what was at stake and what he was giving up. When he opened the door, all I wanted to do was melt into his arms. But Earvin was cold. Distant. He stood practically behind the door as he made way for me to walk into the suite, and then extended his hand toward the couch, beckoning me to sit there. He sat opposite me on the chair. The distance between us felt like it spanned a continent.

"Look, Cookie, I wish I had a better explanation for you, but it really is simple," he said. "I just can't do it."

"But I don't understand," I said, with tears welling. "How could we go from picking out a church and getting the invitations together to breaking up? What did I do wrong? Where did we go wrong?"

"I can't explain it," he said, emotionless. "I'm not doing this to hurt you. I just don't want to get married."

I was quiet—searching for the right words to say. But there were none. I looked down at my left hand and ran the tips of my fingers over the diamonds in my engagement ring. Slowly, I twisted it and dragged it off my finger and dropped it into my palm. I absentmindedly swiped at the tears streaming down my cheeks. "I just want you to know, this is it," I said, sniffling. "When I walk out this door, we're done. Never again. Are you sure this is what you want? You sure you can't tell me why you can't do this?"

"I just can't," he said.

And just like that, it was officially, truly over. After that night, an entire year would pass by without Earvin and I communicating with each other—no phone calls, no letters, no checking in after the games or meet-ups when he came back home for games, holidays, and the off-season. He stayed in his corner of the world, where Magic Johnson was the loud, flashy king, and I stayed in Toledo, quiet. Devastated. Brokenhearted.

· Finding Cookie ·

The pity party was long, sappy, and relentless: it seemed like everyone had something to say about the break off of my engagement to Earvin, and rightfully so, considering he'd made that very public announcement, inviting the entire world into our most intimate space. Holing up in Toledo helped just a bit; at least I didn't have to worry about paparazzi stalking me at the grocery store and the mall, or posting up outside my apartment. Still, for months, I had to wind my way through the pitiful looks everyone from my family to my friends to my coworkers would toss my way the moment I crossed their line of vision. Work was the worst. That first day, I walked into the office, on time but dragging, eyes puffy from a fresh round of inconsolable tears. A hush washed over what had been a bustling conversation and, soon after, came the sad faces and the back rubs and the repeated "Are you okay?" and "How can we help?" questions. I could barely muster an answer. I was having a hard enough time trying to keep myself from having a nervous breakdown; the absolute last thing I needed was unsolicited commentary on how awful Earvin was or how long it would take for me to "get over him."

"See, what you need to do," one coworker said, "is to find yourself a new guy. That's the best cure for a broken heart."

"Or you could just wait it out and see if Magic comes around," another said. "He'll realize what he's missing soon enough."

Somehow, I mustered a halfhearted smile, but it was more for their sake than it was for mine. I knew better. Feeling shattered and worn, the last thing I wanted or needed was to chase after Earvin or, worse, hop into a new relationship. After that, I started getting to work early and hiding in my office all day, keeping busy so that I didn't have to say anything to anyone or, worse, listen to a coworker try to console me whenever I'd break down and cry.

Through the thick of consoling phone calls and visits, only one voice stood out: Angie Aguirre's. She was the wife of Mark Aguirre and part of one of the three NBA couples Earvin and I had become quite close to as we got more serious—someone I considered a good friend, even after Earvin and I broke up. Angie made a point of not only checking in on me but giving me valuable advice on how to save my sanity and get back to living.

"You know," she told me in one particularly introspective phone call that helped put me on the road to recovery, "I went through hell with Mark." She shared her own story of heartbreak and survival.

"Oh my God," I said, sighing as I snuggled under the covers in my bed, where I'd been spending pretty much all of my free time outside of work. "How did you even begin to make it through that?"

"I spent a lot of time on my knees, praying to God to help me and Mark get our act together and work together as a couple," she said. "But what was helpful for me to figure out what *I* wanted and needed to feel whole was going to Bible study."

I sat up in my bed and leaned into the phone's receiver. "Really?" I asked skeptically. "Because I've been going to church, but I haven't felt anything yet."

"You have to get into that Bible," Angie insisted. "That's where you're going to find your strength. It's not about what Earvin wants. It's not about what your mother or sister wants. It's not even about what you want. When you read His word, you're going to learn that all that matters is what God wants."

This was, by no means, a revolutionary concept for me: I knew Jesus. I found Him at the tender age of five, down in Huntsville, Alabama, the small country town where I was born and spent my early childhood. I'll never forget the majesty of baptisms by the river—how the women floated down the streets in their white robes snapping against the wind as they ushered their charges to the water. To my young eyes, it was all at once scary and beautiful. Mesmerizing. Even then, barely in kindergarten, I knew I wanted to be a part of that beauty—that energy and passion that moved like a wave through the lives of the people around me.

I wanted to be a part of that beauty—that energy and passion that moved like a wave through the lives of the people around me.

My parents didn't really go to church save for on special holidays, like Easter and Christmas. But Mrs. Wheeler, a lady who lived across the street, took her two sons every week to Sunday school and church, and invited me to attend with her and her family. "I want you to go to church with us," she said, cupping my face in her hands. "You'll be my little girl."

I was out of breath and sweaty when I ran back across the street, searching for my mother. I needed her to give me permission right away. "Mommy," I said, huffing. "The lady across the street wants me to go to church with her. Can I go? Please?"

"Sure," my mother said.

Every Sunday, my mother would dress me up in my fancy dress and my shiny patent leather Mary Jane shoes and send me across the street. I held tight to Mrs. Wheeler's hand the first time we walked through the large double doors into the sanctuary; the sight of the bright red pulpit and the choir lifting their voices to the rafters was mesmerizing.

"You okay, sugar?" my neighbor asked as we settled into our seats.

"Yes, ma'am," I said slowly, as I took it all in. I didn't understand everything that was going on, but I loved sitting in the sanctuary that morning and every other Sunday after that. You would think that a little five-year-old would be screaming, "I'm hungry! Get me out of here!" But the routine of going to church, feeling that peace in the room, relishing in the community that enveloped us, all of that meant something to me, even as a little girl.

After my father moved our family to Detroit in search of better opportunities and, a few years later, when we moved out of an apartment and into our first home, we lived directly across the street from Northwestern Christian Church. In the summers, my mother signed me up for vacation Bible school. I liked it so much,

I asked if I could start going to Sunday school. I really believe that God had His hand on me and was slowly leading me to Him.

I came to know God on my own in this way and never wavered from His word. But when I followed Angie's advice and searched out a Bible study group that could help me apply His word to my life, I learned that God never left my side, either. Indeed, it was He who got me through.

That night after Angie and I talked, I opened my Bible and read the first thing my eyes focused on; it happened to be the story of Joseph, the dreamer. In the story, God repeatedly gives Joseph dreams that reveal His plans for young Joseph's life, and Joseph, ever the believer, never wavers in his faith that his dreams will come true. He holds on to them, even after his ten older brothers sell him into slavery out of jealousy over their father's love for his youngest son. Joseph trusts God's plans, too, even when, accused of flirting with an officer's wife, he's falsely imprisoned in Egypt. When Joseph correctly predicts that Egypt will have a period of largess, followed by years of famine, the Egyptian pharaoh puts Joseph, once a poor Hebrew, in charge of not only overseeing the lands but also guiding the great nation through the good harvest and the scarcity. Joseph's predictions end up saving Egypt and its people from starvation. Ultimately, his unfaithful brothers are saved, also, when, in search of food, they happen upon Joseph, who not only forgives his brothers' betrayal, but uses his powerful position to stop his family from starving.

Joseph's story couldn't have been more fitting for that very moment in my life. Every time something went wrong, God picked Joseph up, brushed him off, and assured him that he would win—that he would be king someday. And no matter what happened to him, Joseph believed God with his whole heart and stayed faithful to that word. It is what got him through. That amazing story gave me strength—made me understand that crying and being depressed and feeling sorry for myself weren't nearly as effective as trusting that God had a plan for me and that I needed to trust His vision for my life. I didn't need anyone's pity, especially my own. What I needed was to search for God's purpose for me. I needed to get to know God better and put Him first so that He could direct my path.

That focus translated into this: I went to work during the weekdays, Bible study on Wednesdays, and church on Sundays. That was my life. I did have the occasional date here and there, but really, I lived in Toledo, Ohio; the pickings were slim. When my best friend moved to Chicago, I did have access to a larger pool of more eligible bachelors, but dating seriously was not a priority for me—not by a stretch, not for some time.

A few years had passed after my awful breakup with Earvin before I started flirting with the idea of dating again. But, in typical form, as if he had some kind of magic bat signal that sent magnetic waves to his heart when I was dating someone else, Earvin made his presence known again just as I was considering diving back into the dating pool. Earvin's phone calls came infrequently, first; I'd get home from work and find a message on the answering machine. "Just calling to check in on you," he'd say.

Then, one day, I was there to answer the phone.

"Hey, how you doing?" he asked, his voice sweet, cheery.

"I'm fine," I said, a little more tersely than I'm sure he expected. I wasn't sure what he wanted and, frankly, both my dignity and I had recovered enough to harden ourselves from his advances. I wasn't moved by his niceties.

"Well," he said, hesitating a little, "I'm coming to town; we're playing the Pistons. Do you wanna watch the game?"

"Nope."

Earvin was quiet. Finally, he said, "Everything okay with you?"

"I'm good," I said. "How are you? You doing good?"

"I'm great," he said, laughing nervously. "I just figured maybe since I was in town maybe you might want to come watch the game."

"I'm not coming down there," I said, laughing.

We exchanged a few more pleasantries but quickly hung up after that. I was proud of myself; I was getting stronger. Eventually, I got strong enough, even, to check up on him occasionally, particularly, as usual, if he had a hard loss or he got injured. I cared enough about him to do that much without expecting a relationship in return. Then, over the course of six months, those infrequent check-ins turned into what our phone calls used to be:

long, introspective, funny conversations about everything and nothing at all. The kind of conversations shared between two people who had plans for each other.

· Finding Our Way Back ·

I met a man from Chicago who was nice enough and interesting and with whom I got along well. I had my reservations about him; when we met, he said he was separated from his wife, a detail that didn't set right with me. I agreed to date him only after the divorce papers were signed and filed, and, sure enough, when he announced to me that he was free, clear, and really single, I gave a relationship with him a shot. This was a problem for Earvin—that much became clear one evening when he called and I announced that I couldn't talk because I had "company."

"What do you mean you have company?" Earvin asked, a bit of bass in his voice.

"I have company," I said, equal parts annoyed and amused.

"Who's there, Cookie?" Earvin demanded.

"Excuse me, you can't ask me who I'm seeing or who's over here at my house," I whisper yelled into the receiver. *What nerve,* I thought. By then, he was practically gallivanting across the tabloids with some newscaster lady on his arm, and he had the nerve to question whom I was seeing?

"Who's there, Cookie?" Earvin asked again, pressing.

"A friend," I finally offered. "A friend of mine from Chicago that I'm seeing."

"You're seeing somebody?" he asked. Earvin got quiet. Finally, he said, simply, "Oh."

"I have to go now," I said, satisfied that he not only understood the words coming out of my mouth but also that those words made him feel some kind of way.

"Yeah, okay," he said, hanging up the phone shortly thereafter.

A few hours later, Earvin called back. "I'm still with my friend," I said when I picked up the phone.

"Oh, you need to get rid of him," he said.

"Good-bye, Earvin," I said, laughing.

After that night, there were many more phone calls like this, with Earvin checking in and checking on me. I could tell he'd felt something: he was bothered that someone else was staking his claim, yes, but he was also starting to recognize what he'd lost.

Frankly, I was, too.

It was New Year's Eve when I decided it wasn't going to work with "Chicago." I'd flown into the Windy City and met him at my friend's place; from there, we went to a Luther Vandross concert, and followed that with a toast to a new beginning and another year. But rather than start the new year together, I closed our chapter. I'd realized that I was still in love with Earvin, and I needed to figure that out. I didn't think it was fair to Chicago to lead him to think we could go any further.

"Look," I said, "this isn't going to work out."

Confused, Chicago stared for a moment, then said: "What? What's not going to work?"

"You. Me. This isn't going to work," I said. "We have to end this."

"Why?" he asked.

"Because I think I'm in love with somebody else," I said, practically blurting it out. The truth was I didn't have time for Chicago. My heart was in Los Angeles. I needed to go back to Earvin.

The next morning, Earvin called my friend's apartment, where I was staying while bringing in the New Year in Chicago. I'm not sure how Earvin found the number or how he knew I was there, but he was on the other end of the receiver my friend was pushing into my face. "Here we go—back down memory lane. You two back at it, huh?" she said, shaking her head as I grabbed the phone. "Might as well; you can't stay away from each other."

She was right about that. Earvin had called to wish me a Happy New Year, but also to let me know that he'd broken up with the woman he'd been dating. "I want my girl back," he said simply.

I'd spent four years drawing closer to God and preparing myself for something bigger—for what God wanted for me. And God ultimately led me back to Earvin.

Chapter Five

Saying "I Do"

This time around, Earvin and I knew that if we were going to be together, if, after all of our fits and starts, we were going to build a solid relationship looking forward to our future, the long-distance love was not going to work. For Earvin, there was too much at stake: he needed to know if I could fit seamlessly into the physical and mental fortress he'd built as a high-profile, top-performing professional athlete. Understand, this was no small thing: the level of intensity Earvin brought to the court was epic. Before games, he would go into warrior mode, shutting himself off from everything and everyone, studying game tape, sitting in the dark, getting hyped for battle. Nothing and no one else existed: the only thing that mattered to him was destroying his opponent and winning, and he followed a strict code of rules and rituals to up his chances. Always, there was an order to things, and he would be very clear and precise about them: he would wake up at the same time, he would eat the same food, he would wear the same clothing, go to bed the night before a game at the same time, and arrive at the stadium, always before the rest of his teammates. Like a man governed by superstitions, everything he touched had to have its place. Over the course of his career, there was no room for variations, and definitely no room for another person in Magic's war room. We both agreed that the only way to see if I could fit into his life was for me to move to California and become a part of his rituals—to cheer for him from the family section at the games, to be the one waiting for him outside the locker room when he was finished on the court, to be the one holding his hand at NBA functions, special dinners, and celebrations with his friends and mine, too. Living in Toledo and seeing Earvin only occasionally made it much too difficult to be a part of his world, and if I wasn't included in the ritual, it would never, ever work. And so both of us made the very grown-up decision to be together in the same place so that I could insert myself into his life routine and, by extension, his game routine.

I didn't want to lose my independence and my identity. Moving across the country to be with Earvin in Los Angeles required me to give up a good job back in Toledo and, frankly, I was afraid of the implications. After all, I'd made inroads in my career doing what I loved, and uprooting my life to take a chance to see if we had what it took to get married was scary. If it didn't work out, what would I have to fall back on? Where was my security? I uprooted myself, my life, my comfort. What's more, my moving to California made Earvin nervous, too, because until then, he'd spent a decade living his life exactly as he pleased, and now, he, too, would have to make some serious adjustments. With all of this in mind, the two of us agreed that Earleatha Kelly would depend on herself until we figured out how to move forward together. That meant living in my own apartment, driving the car I purchased with my own money—an old but reliable gold Honda—and getting my own job so that I could continue to excel in the career I'd worked so hard to get.

With that, Earvin and I put the past behind us, starting with a clean slate and intentions to be a part of each other's lives on a daily basis. It sounds so simple, but with the majority of our relationship played out over long distance, being together was a big deal. Earvin could see me *in* his life. I was adjusting to a whole new lifestyle, and he was relishing in all that came with the solid relationship we were building: the money and flash meant nothing compared to the simplest joys we found in going to Fat Burger after the games, lounging around at the house, spending time with our families when they were in town. All the things that brought us to each other back in college provided the glue that would bind us. What's more, Earvin also quickly realized that having someone there for him to celebrate the wins and comfort him after losses was an advantage, not a hindrance—something he never even realized he needed because he'd never had someone there for him like that before.

From time to time, we jokingly brought up marriage. "You know," I said, one evening while I cooked dinner for Earvin at his house, "I could never live here with you."

"What do you mean?" he asked, frowning. I could see him making calculations in his head, perhaps thinking that I didn't want to live in a space that had history and memories of times he had with his exes and other women he'd been with. That wasn't it, though.

"You've lived here for so long, Earvin," I said, turning down the fire under the saucepan and putting the spoon in its cradle. "This is your space, and if I move in here, I'd be invading that space. We need to start fresh so that we are both moving into a house to start our lives together, as one."

Earvin was quiet for a moment. "You're right," he said.

"Really?" I said, excitedly.

"Yeah, we can start looking for a place, soon," he said.

Not long after that, we began building a home—the one that we live in to this day. It was almost ready for us to move into right around the 1990 All-Star Weekend in Miami, when the East bested the West 130–113, with Earvin taking home the MVP trophy, so our excitement was palpable, made so not only by the festivities, but also by the presence of Earvin's family and mine, both of which he'd invited to the game. We had an incredible time watching Earvin make magic on the court, but the real fun came later that evening, when Earvin arranged for our entire family—our parents and his siblings—to have dinner at a little hole-in-the-wall soul food restaurant he'd shut down for the evening just for us. I was too busy enjoying my dinner and the company we were keeping to realize what Earvin had up his sleeve. Suddenly, he stood up and began clinking his fork on his water glass to get everyone's attention. *What's he doing?* I thought as I sipped my water.

"I love Cookie so much," Earvin said, standing there, his shoulders squared, his tall, lanky body filling the space. "She left a good job and the bright lights of Toledo, Ohio, to move to Los Angeles to be with me, and I love her for loving me. I'm in love with her."

A rush of "awwwwwws" filled the room. Then Earvin reached into his pocket, pulled out a tiny box, and handed it to me. "Cookie," he said, "will you marry me?"

Now, I saw the first ring coming because everyone around us was getting married and our joining in on the "getting hitched" wagon made sense then. But this proposal I didn't see coming. I was happy for it, though. Finally, after spending a year together in the same city on a daily basis, I felt like we'd grown—like we really fit together. I wanted nothing more than to marry him, and here he was, declaring in front of everyone we loved that he wanted nothing more than to marry me. "Yes," I said, smiling and excited. "Yes, I'll marry you."

We started planning right away, this time plotting a much more low-key ceremony in Lansing, so that, rather than having to deal with the media spectacle that was sure to cloud our day, we could focus on celebrating each other and our love. It looked like everything was going to go off without a hitch: the invitations were ready to be shipped, my dress was on its way from New York, we'd secured the perfect church for the ceremony, and his sisters and I were bonding over the planning, with which they were helping.

And then Earvin dropped the bomb. Again.

"I can't do it," he said.

• Limping to the Altar •

Nothing had happened—we hadn't had a fight, neither of us was seeing anyone else on the sly, no one had even remotely, to my knowledge, tried to throw a cog in the wheel by suggesting that maybe we weren't right for each other. We were in the car, sitting outside my apartment in Los Angeles after having just come back from lunch, and Earvin just turned to me and broke off our engagement.

This time, though, I didn't get upset. I got annoyed. "What are you talking about?" I said. "What is wrong with you?"

"I just can't do it," he said, lying back in the driver's seat, running his hands over his face. "Look, you need to give me the ring back."

"Nope," I said, easily. "We're not doing this again." Earvin sat there, alternately staring at my ring and at me as I absentmindedly fiddled with the diamond. "If you don't want to get married right now, fine. We can cancel the wedding. But we're staying engaged. I will not go through this again, with everybody pitying me and me going crazy wondering what I did wrong. You cannot humiliate me again."

"But I can't do it," was all Earvin could muster. "We have to break the engagement."

"You're not getting this ring back, and it's not coming off my finger," I said, shrugging.

We kept on like that, arguing back and forth, for what seemed like an eternity until, finally, I'd had enough and got out of the car and stomped into my apartment. Now I was angry and frustrated on top of annoyed. Still, I knew that, deep down, he loved me, and I understood what was going on: every time we got to that part of the planning stage when it was feeling real to him, Earvin freaked out. The specter of having to rearrange his rituals to incorporate me into his life was just too much, and rather than march forward with me, he ran.

But I wasn't about to give up on Earvin. On us. And I certainly wasn't going to let him get away with breaking another engagement.

So I forced him back into his routine—the one that included me. I'd call him and say, "Okay, see you at the game, hon," and then I'd show up like all was well. I'd call him, too, to ask what would be our dinner plans. I proceeded as if everything were normal. Earvin would try to ignore me and then, when he realized I wasn't going anywhere, he'd whisper into my ear jokingly: "Give me that ring."

"Nope," I'd say, just as calm and cool.

We went on like this for a good while, until he loosened up and got over whatever was bugging him. He stopped asking me for the ring and began initiating conversations again, almost as if nothing had happened, and eventually, we fell back into our old routines. No doubt, he felt guilty, and he set about making things right. One night, he even invited a bunch of our friends and me to dinner at a hot new restaurant that was getting a lot of buzz in the press. "I have something to do before then, so just meet me there," he said. I said, "Okay," and thought nothing more of it beyond a sigh of relief and joy that we were back on again.

When dinner was over, I walked out to the valet and waited with one of my girlfriends, Gina, while our cars were retrieved from the parking lot. Not long after, the man who took my ticket pulled up in a black Porsche. He hustled out of the car and over to me: "Here's your keys," he said cheerily.

"No, no, that's not my car," I said, shaking my head. "I mean, it would be nice if that was my car," I chuckled in my girlfriend's direction. "But that's not my car. I'm in the gold Honda."

Confused, the valet looked at me and then at the keys, then hustled himself away to find my car. I was glancing at my watch, wondering just where he'd gone with my ride when the valet finally walked back up, this time with another man by his side. In the man's hands was a folder of papers: title and registration and insurance cards and a few more items. "This is your car," he said, pointing at the papers. My name was on the title. "Look!"

As I leaned into the paperwork, I caught a glimpse of Earvin in the background, cracking up. Gina caught on and started laughing, too. "Oh my God, he got you a Porsche!" she screamed.

I giggled, too, as I looked at the car and then at Earvin. I think Earvin realized he'd made a mistake and this was his way of making up for it without coming out and actually saying it.

We were back on again.

When the playoffs were in sight, Earvin flipped the script on me again, but this time in a good way. "Cookie," he said to me one day, "the playoffs are starting. Do you want to come on the road with us?"

"Really? I can come?" I asked, surprise ringing my voice.

"Yeah, I asked you, so do you want to come?"

"Yeah."

I was shocked. Shocked. Because not once in his entire basketball career—from college through his time with the Lakers— had Earvin ever invited me to support him on the road at a playoff game. He'd tried to invite me a couple times, but always, just days before the start of the series, his agent would call and give an excuse for why I wouldn't be able to attend the games. Always, there'd be some kind of sound explanation: the coach didn't want wives present, or Earvin needed to focus on the game rather than worrying about me. I think Earvin would get nervous at the last minute because he felt like he couldn't focus on the game and worry about me at the same time. My very presence would throw off the ritual.

But this time felt different.

"I'd love to," I said, trying to temper my excitement in case he got nervous and changed his mind again.

Going to the playoffs came with stipulations, though, which Earvin was quick to lay out. "If you come, know this: you can't stay with me, you can't fly with me, you can't even be in the same hotel as me. You gotta stay with one of the other wives or girl-friends." The coach didn't want any distractions for the players.

"Okay," I quickly agreed.

The first series was against the Golden State Warriors, and my friend Sharon Drew, Larry Drew's wife, graciously agreed to be my roommate and show me the ropes. The wives and girlfriends moved like a squad, eating together, traveling together, sitting in the same section to root our men on. We were something else, strutting into the stadium, dressed in all white to make clear that we were the significant others, there to support the Lakers, but also to easily signal our support to the players. My legs shook as we walked into the enemy's lair; they led us to a tiny little section surrounded by a sea of gold and blue—Warriors colors. "Wow," was all I could muster. "This is intense."

Then, all of a sudden, the lights went out and spotlights began to flash as loud rap music blared through the booming sound system. The announcer shouted the starting lineup's names into the mic, all an elaborate setup to introduce Tim Hardaway, Mitch Richmond, and Chris Mullin, the killer Golden State trio that was so lethal and popular on the court that they actually started referring to themselves as "Run TMC," a take on the hit rap trio that, at the time, was ruling the charts, Run-DMC.

The crowd roared. All we could do was sit in silence, tight-faced, and then cheer until we were hoarse when the Lakers took the floor. I can't lie: it was intimidating but quite a rush. The Lakers went on to massacre Run TMC in that series, and, after that, the Portland Trail Blazers, too, and, for the first time, I got to ride shotgun with Earvin as he celebrated the wins. "It's the Lakers up in here!" he'd lead the team in chanting. I felt like a schoolgirl watching the star of the basketball team pound his chest after a win, and loved when, sweaty, heart racing, happy, he would take my hand, his actions making a very calculated, public declaration that I was, indeed, the love of his life.

He'd made his choice to be with me, but when it was time for the finals against Chicago, I would be forced to make a hard decision for our relationship, too. See, that series came exactly at the same time as the busiest season at my job: market week. My bosses were two ladies who had been gracious enough to allow me the time off to traipse to Oakland and Portland to watch the Golden State and Trail Blazers games. But they needed me on their three-person team for market week, when we were charged with divvying up the stores and taking their representatives all around Los Angeles to check out the merchandise we were recommending they sell in their establishments. The implications of my taking off from work at that specific time would be huge and, frankly, could lead to me losing my job. Still, not going to the games had consequences, too: essentially, I would be telling Earvin that my job was more important than my support for him.

I was torn, but I took the risk and asked for the time off anyway, hoping for a best-case scenario: my bosses would divvy up my work among themselves and let me have the time off to show Earvin that my support for him was unequivocal. Yeah, it didn't go over so well.

"Oh, no, absolutely not," my one boss said when I nervously made the inquiry. "This is market week—you can't go anywhere. We need you here."

"I understand," I said quietly, dejected. "You're absolutely right: it's market week. I need to be here."

But I spent many a moment after that stressed and anxious. After all, I had a ring, but we still had no concrete marriage plans. We weren't raising a family together. And I'd worked so hard to excel in my career; I was serious about my job and my independence. My paycheck was paying my way and made it so that if things didn't work out with Earvin, I could still depend on myself to be my own separate entity, capable of paying my own bills, buying my own place, living my own life. I wasn't in Los Angeles pretending to work hard so that Earvin would respect me and ask me to marry him. The last thing I wanted to do was to let my bosses down.

• An Uneasy Choice •

Still, ultimately, I wanted to be with Earvin—to be a part of his life at that particular moment. Earvin and I had great momentum and, for the first time, he was inviting me into this part of his life. This was big for us.

Depressed and uncertain about which to choose, I stated my case to Earvin. He was clear, understanding, and direct: "You can go to the championship games if you want to go, but I would never jeopardize your job," he said. "It's on you. I got it set up; if you want to go, it's done. If you don't, it's cool. I'll see you when I get back. I'm not going to make that decision for you."

That, of course, was absolutely no help to me. In fact, it made the decision even more challenging, because he was being quite clear in communicating his desire to include me in his world—at the moment that was more important to him. Never before, in the twelve years that we'd been dating, engaged, and making plans together had he invited me into his space in this way. That he asked me was a *big deal*. Not just for me—but for him, especially.

Though he wasn't pressuring me, I literally went back and forth for days about what to do, and even hit up my most trusted girlfriends and family members for their advice. Earvin's agent's wife, Laurie, wasted no time giving me her sound advice: "I work, too, so I understand what you're saying here. But I would go," she insisted. In a separate phone call, Sharon was equally firm: "Cookie, you know what? You've gotten this far, and this is important to him. If he invited you to go, it's important, trust me. You better get on that plane to Chicago."

I was up the entire night before the first game, still unsure of what to do, scared to make a decision, weighing the options. I literally let it go until the last possible second. Ultimately, it was my gut that made the decision: *Go*, it was telling me. *Earvin invited you to the games because he wants you there, but he also wants to see if he can handle you being there. He needs to make you a part of the ritual.* Ultimately, I had to see for myself that he could manage playing at the top of his game with me front and center, a permanent part of his life both on and off the court.

That phone call to my bosses letting them know I was choosing my man over my job was one of the hardest phone calls I'd ever had to make. I was sobbing when one of my bosses answered my call. "I'm so sorry for doing this to you," I said through my sniffles. "I love you guys and you've been so good to me. I wouldn't be doing this if I didn't absolutely have to. You know how up and down our relationship is," I continued. "I would never disrespect you guys, and I need you to know that my going isn't about you, it's about Earvin and me."

"I understand," she said, her voice warm. "But you know you're fired, right? Do what you have to do, but when you come back, clean out your office."

She was right to fire me—I knew that. I spent the next few minutes helping her strategize how to cover all the work I was leaving behind for her and her partner, and then the next hour after that, packing my suitcase, rushing to the airport, and bawling over the fact that I'd let my bosses down and, to some extent, myself, too. I had chosen a relationship over my career. I prayed that entire four-hour flight that I hadn't made a mistake.

It was God who confirmed for me that I made the right decision: when I stepped off that plane, Earvin was standing there with his parents, waiting for me with open arms.

"It's so good to see you!" I said to his mother as I folded myself into her warm embrace.

"I'm so glad you came," she said.

She was right about that. It was good for the three of us to be seen in the stands at Earvin's championship games, and here's why: never before in Earvin's ten-year career in the NBA had he ever invited his parents to the finals, either. It was a special moment for Earvin, for me, for family. For all of us. We were all witnessing Earvin's growth—his maturation into a new head-space that was bigger than just him. Finally, he was starting to get comfortable melding the brute, glitzy world of Magic Johnson with the steady, simple family-man life Earvin had long craved, and he could see me in it.

· Finally, a Wedding ·

The finals against Chicago were a bust; Michael Jordan led the Bulls to a 4–1 series victory over what would be Earvin's last champion-ship run. Still, we were riding high, Earvin and I; despite the phenom-enal loss of the last game played in Los Angeles, our relationship was on a winning streak.

He was starting to get comfortable melding the brute, glitzy world of Magic Johnson with the steady, simple family-man life Earvin had long craved, and he could see me in it.

Now, I was fully aware of Earvin's annual post-playoffs respite to the Bahamas: for years, he'd gone to the Caribbean to recover from the physical and mental brutality that came with being a professional bas-ketball player. For weeks, he would subsist on pure adrenaline; he'd barely eat, sleep was elusive, and he stayed dehydrated from the level of play he'd employ chasing that championship ring. It was awful to watch: his skin would turn gray, he'd lose a ton of weight, he'd be cranky. A solo vacation centered on peace, quiet, and rest was his personal prescription for championship-series recovery, and I never, ever questioned his desire to get away. He needed it.

What he didn't need, though, was the annual pool party he'd planned to throw the weekend before leaving for his trip—a notorious soiree that I didn't know he hosted at his home until I started getting phone calls from my Laker wives friends. Apparently, they felt some kind of way about them, and they figured since I was now officially incorporated into Laker world, I should not only know the sordid details of what, exactly, was happening at my man's party but also have the power to stop it. Their insistence that I do something about it was consistent and relentless: "What you need to do is tell him that party is off, hence now and forevermore," one said. Another gave me the wretched details of what she heard went down: "There's a bikini contest, strippers, and a whole lot of groupies crawling all over our men." Yet a third wife made it plain: "If the wives can't go to this party, you know they're doing all kinds of things they shouldn't be doing. You need to end that, stat."

I wasted not one second getting Earvin on the phone to relay what I'd heard, and he was even quicker on the draw with some NFL tackle-worthy pushback of his own. "It's just a pool party," he said, sounding annoyed and a tad groggy after waking up from a nap to answer my call. "What are you talking about?"

"Well, if it's just a party, then I'm coming," I said confidently, throwing down the gauntlet.

"No, you can't come."

"What do you mean I can't come, Earvin? Why can't I come to my fiancé's party?"

"I always have these parties and they're for guys, Cookie," he said, becoming more annoyed by the second.

"You know what that says to me, Earvin?" I asked, leaning into the phone, my face turning red with a combination of frustration and anger. "If the wives can't come, then you must be doing something that none of us would like. I mean, if you're not doing anything wrong, why can't the wives come?"

"Because it's just a bunch of guys hanging out!" he snapped.

"And the girls in the bikinis. Don't forget about the girls in the bikinis. You can't have the bikini contest without them. They're not guys," I yelled.

We argued back and forth—me accusing, him defending—with neither one of us budging, but getting increasingly angry with each other. Finally, I did it: I pulled the marriage card. "Earvin, you can't do this: we're engaged," I said quietly. "We're going to get married soon. You can't have one of these parties in a space that we've built together. It's not right."

"I'm having the party, Cookie, and we don't have to get married."

The next thing I heard was the dial tone.

I stared at the phone, gently placed it back in the cradle, and let the hot tears run down my cheeks, across my face, and settle on my neck and shirt. Out of the corner of my eye, I caught a tiny glimpse of my wedding dress hanging in my bedroom closet, a sight that made me burst into a full-on scream. *What did you just do?* I kept asking myself. *What are you going to do?* Like a reoccurring nightmare that I just couldn't shake, this man had again tossed me and all that we'd built together into a heap, as if our love were this disposable thing he could throw away when it lacked the proper luster, or didn't taste how he'd expected, or didn't work to his exact specifications.

Except I wasn't a thing. I was his woman, a person with a heart that beat and feelings that mattered and emotions that just couldn't take any more of this on-again, off-again manipulation. Truly, I was lost—most certainly scared. After all, just a few weeks before, I made the conscious decision to forget all the other times he'd called it quits on a whim and to throw away everything I held dear, including my job and my autonomy, to be with this man— all so that I could choose *us*. And that meant nothing: I was back to square one, but even worse off than before: this time, I had no job, no means of paying my rent, a car that I owned but that he bought, and so much embarrassment about the entire situation that I couldn't even bring myself to tell anyone, besides Adrianne, about the latest breakup. "Maybe I can move to Alaska," I told my best friend. "I want to go live with the Eskimos. They'll let me sit in the dark all day, and they won't hurt me. It's cold, but I'll be safe."

I called Earvin back several times that day and every day after that in tears, asking him the same question: "You're still having that party?"

"Get off my phone, Cookie. Yes, I'm still having my party."

I even talked to him on the morning the whole affair was going down and inquired again. Earvin wouldn't budge. "Would you stop?" he yelled into the phone as I sobbed. "What is wrong with you? I'm just having a party. I don't understand why you're making such a big deal out of this."

"But—" I began.

"Would you just shut up? I'm getting off this phone."

Dial tone. Again.

That's it, I said to myself. I'm done. I rushed over to my kitchen counter, snatched the morning paper off it, and then plopped down at my dining room table and thumbed through the want ads. I was on a mission: there would be no more sitting around crying over Earvin Johnson. I was going to focus on Cookie again—this time, for good.

Three days would pass before Earvin called again, this time from his hotel room in the Bahamas. "Are you still crying?"

"No," I said with attitude—like a woman who didn't care anymore. I could tell my simple statement threw him.

"Well," he stuttered, "I don't know, I've had a few days to get some rest and think about us, and I wanted to call you to tell you that I think I can get married."

I hadn't seen that one coming. "What?" I asked, confused. "What do you mean?"

"Cookie," he explained, "this was the best thing for me, to just come down here by myself to really think about things. I thought about a lot. I had the best time with you during the play-offs and the finals. It was the first time that I knew you could be in that world, and I was happy to witness it. It didn't bother me to have you there, and I was still able to play at the level we played at without being distracted. I realized that your being there had nothing to do with us losing. Your being there was okay. I think the two of us being together will be okay."

My gut was telling me to call him an idiot for doubting me—for doubting us. My heart wasn't as strong; it simply wanted to tap out. "I'm done," I told Earvin quietly. "I can't marry you. I can't do this anymore. I'm not planning another wedding, I'm not picking another dress, I'm not having more invitations made up so that they can sit by the door and you can call it quits again. I'm a basket case. You refuse to understand that—"

Earvin cut me off. "What do I need to do?" he said. "I want us to be together."

"You want to be together?" I asked, huffing. At that moment, I decided, I needed to put my foot down and issue the ultimatum. "Really? How about this: you get on a plane right now and you come back to Los Angeles. We'll go to Vegas the very next day and we'll handle that. If you don't want to go to Vegas, then the courthouse it is. I don't have a problem with that, either. But if you're going to say you want to be married, we're getting married right away."

Earvin chuckled. "No, you deserve a wedding after all this. I'm going to give you a wedding."

"Nope," I insisted. "We don't need a spectacle. If you want, we can throw a big party afterward, but what I want is to be married—now. Before you change your mind again."

"I can't do that to you," he insisted. "Don't worry. I promise we're going to get married. Let me handle it. You still got your dress, right?"

"Yeah, I have my dress," I said.

"All right, the only thing we don't have is the cake. I'm going to have my sisters call the cake lady right now . . ."

Maybe this is what Earvin needed to get down the aisle—to be the point guard in the planning. All I know is that after all that needless drama, after yet another split, he plotted and planned, with the help of his sisters, a beautiful ceremony and reception that required only two things from me: to get the bridesmaids' dresses and to show up to the church—a sanctuary in Lansing that his father attended—in my white dress.

I showed up to the church two hours before the ceremony because Earvin warned me that if I was late (which I always am), he would not get married. I looked beautiful but was a total wreck. An hour before the ceremony, Earvin, who'd spent the morning with his parents, was nowhere to be found. I was on the border of a total meltdown when his mother walked into the tiny dressing area where my hairstylist was fussing over my curls; Earvin was supposed to ride to the church with his mother, but she arrived alone, which alarmed me. "You didn't bring him with you?" I asked.

"Calm down, honey. He's coming," she assured me. "I just talked to him. He'll be here."

Finally, someone peeked through the door and said, "Earvin's in the building." I was grateful for the heads-up; I had to know that he was physically present and, what's more, not looking to deliver to me a "we need to talk" speech about how he couldn't and wouldn't get married on that day.

That speech never came.

Instead, I intertwined my arm with my father's and stood in the vestibule of that church, waiting for Roberta Flack and Donny Hathaway's duet, "The Closer I Get to You," our song, to stream through the speakers. When the music began to play and the double doors to that church swung open, my father turned to me and asked, "Okay, Cookie, you ready to go?"

It was a rhetorical question, but the truth was, at that very moment, I wasn't ready. My legs froze; finally, it dawned on me that this marriage was really going to happen, and all of a sudden, I got scared. It wasn't until I laid eyes on Earvin, the man I'd loved for more than a decade, standing there, wide-eyed and grinning, his heart open and ready to receive the love that I'd saved just for him, that I knew everything was going to be all right. I took one step, and then another, and then another after that, moving closer to the man who would be my husband, more confident with each stride. Then, just as I passed the third pew from the front, my friend Sharon burst into a loud boohoo cry. I knew what her tears were about; she knew all the ups and downs of my relationship with Earvin, and her cry was a loud exaltation that, finally, after all the back-and-forth and ups and downs, the love of my life was finally committing to forever with me. And when she burst into tears, I did, too.

Sharon wasn't the only one bawling that day. Happy tears flowed all through the sanctuary—tears of joy. Finally, love was in control.

Chapter Six

Standing by My Man

That night after Earvin walked through the front door of our home and told me he had the virus that causes AIDS, after I slapped his face for encouraging me to leave him, after I swore to remain steadfast in my vow to stay by his side through sickness and in health, after we fell to our knees and prayed to God to give us the strength to fight for his very life, we hugged and sobbed and held on to each other as if the earth and life and all of time stood still. In the first moments of his revelation, that is what our new reality felt like: silence and darkness. Numbness. In just one moment, our world, this perfect union we'd fought so hard and so long to have, was obliterated, and neither of us had the bandwidth to feel anything but complete and utter shock.

It seemed like an eternity passed before Earvin and I found the strength to unwrap ourselves from each other, wipe our tears, and stand on our own. Still, our heads hung heavy. Then, almost simultaneously, our eyes landed on my belly, full of life. Our baby was there, and that reality knocked us right out of the numbness and deep into the fear.

"Oh my God," I said, wrapping my stomach—our child—in my arms. Staring at my belly, Earvin choked through his sobs: "If anything happened to you and the baby, I just don't know what I would do."

I had no response for that. No salve for either of us. Forget what you know about HIV now, and think back with me to 1991. In those days, there was no talk of powerful antiretroviral treatments, no stories of those who'd survived the disease for decades. The word *HIV* conjured one clear and dreadful thought: *You are going to die.* I'm not talking about the kind of slow and peaceful passing for which loved ones have time to gather and say their good-byes. In the minds of most people, including mine, HIV and AIDS were basically synonymous. Both meant you had days, weeks or, at the most, maybe months left to live. But you certainly didn't have years. And anyone who'd ever so much as touched an HIV-infected person, let alone had sex with him? Well, the assumption was that they were sick and in danger of dying, too. In that moment, then, when we both thought beyond Earvin's diagnosis and considered the implications for our entire growing

family, we were sure the three of us—Earvin, the baby I was carrying in my belly, and I—were in grave danger.

We stood right there, frozen—too scared and broken even
to move. It was sheer will and the might of angels that gave us
the strength finally to make it upstairs to our bedroom, where
we hugged and cried until, physically, mentally, and emotionally
drained, we finally fell asleep.

While Earvin was just as scared as I was, he dealt with his initial fear by shifting into warrior mode. I'd barely wiped the sleep
out of my eyes when he walked into our bedroom and announced
that he'd made an appointment with his doctor for the baby and
me to be tested, and for him to get a second test to confirm his own
diagnosis. "We have to be there on Tuesday at eleven sharp," he
said, buzzing around the room, gathering his clothes from the
dresser and the closet, in a zone.

I wanted him to slow down—to take a beat and explain it all,
not only to give my nerves some semblance of calm, but also to
get some reassurance that maybe this thing wasn't so bad. That
the three of us had a fighting chance.

"What does all of this mean?" I asked quietly, as I swung my
legs over the side of the bed and sat up. "How will this work?"

"How will what work?" Earvin asked, stopping, finally, to
speak.

"The blood test. How does it work and when will we know
for sure if the baby and I are okay?"

"We'll find all that out at the doctor. All those questions, we have to save for the doctor. I just don't know the answers."

"Okay," was all that I could muster.

Throughout the rest of the weekend, Earvin and I sat frozen, silent, uneasy—waiting and talking to no one, save Earvin's agent, Lon, and my friend, Sharon, who called each day to check on us and lend their ears. We wanted to hold the news close to our chests until we made it to the doctor's office. The closest we got to normalcy was watching the Lakers game on television that weekend, which seemed like a good idea until the players filed on to the court for pregame drills and the announcers offered up commentary on why Earvin wasn't on the court. "Magic Johnson, who was out for the game against Utah, is still recovering from the flu and jet lag, we're told," the announcer said confidently. Earvin and I shifted uncomfortably in our chairs but said nothing. In that instant, we both recognized our lives were morphing into something unrecognizable.

Still, Earvin, ever the fighter, refused to let the diagnosis stop him. In fact, it seemed to fuel him. Within three days of discovering he had the virus, he'd connected with Elizabeth Glaser, the prominent AIDS activist married to the actor Paul Michael Glaser, who'd starred in *Starsky & Hutch*. She'd contracted HIV through a blood transfusion and then unknowingly transmitted the disease to her daughter through breastfeeding; a few years later, her second child, a son, became infected in the womb. "There's so much misinformation out there," Elizabeth told Earvin on the evening we visited her. She was so feisty, this tiny little woman, with a conviction that was inspiring. We thought when we went to her house that she would tell Earvin to hang in there. Silly us. "Folks think you can only have AIDS if you're gay or you use infected needles to get high," she continued. "Nobody sees it as a heterosexual disease. You have to be the face of this, a forefather in making people see that anyone can get it. We really need you in this fight, Magic. You've got some work to do."

Elizabeth's fervor gave my husband something to focus on—something other than sickness and an untimely death. "People need to know that you can be heterosexual and get this disease," he kept saying in the days after our meeting with Elizabeth. "We have to save as many lives as possible."

I knew he was right, and I appreciated that Earvin was finding his purpose and crafting a new mission. But really, I was still in my own personal hell, waiting for my blood test results. Unlike today, where one can purchase an HIV test from the local drugstore, and, within minutes, find out your status, I had to wait twelve days to learn my fate, and I was being smothered by fear and uncertainty. Every morning, I would wake up in a panic, worried that I, too, might be HIV-positive and die or worse, that my baby would be sick and not make it. The stress coursed through my veins like a poison, occupying practically every moment of my day. I needed more than a meeting with an activist; I needed to turn directly to God.

As it happened, the West Angeles Church of God in Christ was having a weeklong revival, a perfect refuge to lay down my burdens and talk to the Lord. Though Sharon wasn't a church member, she graciously agreed to drive me and sit by my side while I gathered the spiritual sustenance I needed to carry me through. The congregation was in full praise and worship mode as we pushed through the huge wooden doors and found our way to two empty seats in the sanctuary. Before I could even settle in, the spirit in that room washed over me like a balm. "Oh my Lord, Lord, Lord, Lord!" the choir sang, their robes gently swaying as they clapped and shook their tambourines to the thunder of the organ. When the reverend, a guest preacher I'd never seen there, invited those in need of prayer to the altar for a special prayer, I headed to the front of the church. The preacher was floating among the parishioners, laying hands on those whose tears and furrowed brows betrayed their troubles, when his eyes settled on me. Slowly, he walked my way and looked me eye to eye, as if he were staring into my soul. He pressed his palm on my forehead as he leaned in and talked directly in my ear: "Don't you worry," he said. "God's going to take care of you. Don't you worry. Whatever's going on, know that Jesus is the answer, and you are safe in His arms."

When he said that, a peace like I'd never known washed over me. God led that man to me to deliver that powerful message—

to let me know that I needed to leave my stress and worry in His hands. Before the words could finish flowing out of that pastor's mouth, I knew that God had my back—he wasn't going to leave me alone. I left that sanctuary lifted, armed with the sword I needed to fight what would be the toughest battle of our lives. *God's got it.* That was my mantra. I didn't know how He was going to help us, I didn't know when or from where that help would come, but I knew He was not going to leave me alone and that He would take care of me and Earvin. All I had to do was stay steadfast in His word and have faith. I came out of that church on my own mission, with my challenges straightforward and clear: First, I'd have to figure out how to take care of my husband, who was facing the battle of his life. Second, I had to fortify myself while I waited for the news of my status. Finally, I had to will myself to stay as calm as possible, because freaking out could very well hurt my baby. Just leave the rest to God.

It was this that I held on to in the days leading up to the moment we were to learn our family's fate. I couldn't count on my mother for that, or my father, or my sister, or even Earvin, for that matter; both our families were aware and worried and calling to check in on us and express their support, of course, but conversations with them, while important and necessary in such a close-knit clan, consisted mostly of us consoling them rather than them consoling us. I couldn't count how many times between us Earvin and I said, "No, Mom, really, it's going to be okay," and "Yes, Dad, we're getting the best doctors we can find," and "Absolutely, we are taking care of each other and getting our rest." But really, those words were hollow. I needed to tap into a higher power greater than us all.

The day we got our test results, my heart was pounding so hard I could feel it in my eardrum. Like the most acute tunnel vision, my eyes focused on the manila folder splayed on the leather desktop, my name neatly typed on the tab. There, on a sheet in that folder, was my fate and the fate of my baby.

"Well," the doctor said, walking into the office and circling around to his chair across from us, "I have good news, and I have bad news. The bad news is that Earvin is HIV-positive; his blood test confirms that." I grabbed Earvin's hand and rubbed it between my own. "As for you, Cookie," the doctor said, "both you and the baby are HIV-negative. There is no trace of the virus in your blood."

The rest of what that doctor had to say was a blur; there was talk of getting a team of the top HIV and AIDS doctors in the country to care for Earvin and, of course, details on the medication Earvin would have to take to fight the virus, and a warning for us to use protection every time we had intercourse to reduce my risk of getting infected. The doctor pointed out, too, that the virus could have been lurking in Earvin's system for as long as ten years, and there was really no way to pinpoint when he got it or who he'd gotten it from. "This isn't necessarily the result of some kind of affair he may have had last month," the doctor said. "I need you to understand that part, Cookie." I understood it, but really, it was hard to focus on those details, which, by then, were irrelevant to me. I was too busy trying to balance the sheer joy of our baby and me being healthy with the confirmation of the devastating news that my husband had what we considered poison coursing through his veins.

We had been praying for a specific miracle for the three of us, but God had something else in mind.

· *The Announcement* ·

The afternoon my husband told the world he was HIV-positive, I wore white. I'd picked out my suit the night before, searching through my closet to find just the right outfit for the press conference. *Nothing too dark*, I thought as I searched through the racks of suits in my closet. *No color that whispers death.* I wanted everyone— the players, coaches, owners, and press in the room, and the viewers

> *I wanted everyone to be clear that my husband and I had no plans whatsoever to lie down and die.*

watching us on television—to look at my husband and me and see life. I wanted everyone to be clear that my husband and I had no plans whatsoever to lie down and die.

I won't say putting on this brave front was easy. In fact, when Earvin told me his plans to hold that press conference, just days after his diagnosis was confirmed, I wasn't brave about it at all.

"What? Nooooo," I said, shaking my head violently. "We're not ready for that."

"Oh, I'm going to have a press conference," he insisted, his voice even, measured. "First of all, I need to tell my teammates and everybody why I'm not playing, because there's too many rumors flying around. I just need to say it out loud. Then I'm going to start a foundation to help people understand this disease, and I'm going to fight it with everything I got. I've already planned it, so get your outfit ready."

"Please," I begged him, my eyes flooding with tears. "Can't we just wait?" No amount of time would get me ready. On a basic level, I understood and respected that Earvin was doing what he thought he was called to do, but emotionally, I was a wreck just thinking about the repercussions of going public. Deep in my gut, I was convinced that whatever time my husband had left, he—and by extension, our family—would be stigmatized. Treated like lepers. Turned away at restaurants. We would be subjected to a whole level of crazy, with strangers saying horrible things to us. Even our friends would stop inviting us over, I was convinced. That's why I was so desperate to keep our news a secret. "Why can't we just keep this to ourselves for now, until we get used to it?"

"No," Earvin said forcefully, looking me dead in the eyes. "I have to save as many lives as possible. This is not just about me."

And that was the end of that discussion. Earvin had decided and, as his wife, who'd vowed just two months earlier to stand by him "for better or for worse," I had to follow my husband's lead, no matter how unsure my footing.

On the morning of the press conference, I went to the salon to get my hair done. My hairdresser noticed I was a lot more quiet than usual, so she leaned toward me and whispered, "What's wrong, Cookie?" I couldn't hold it in. As the tears flowed, I told her what everyone on the planet would hear several hours later. "Earvin is HIV-positive," I said through my sobs. Without a word, she came and sat right down beside me, took my hand in hers, and cried right along with me.

By the time I put on my white suit, I was completely numb. Earvin and I were silent on the car ride to the Forum in Inglewood. I avoided conversation because I knew I'd burst into tears if I spoke; I also wanted to give my husband a chance to get his head together. Before the announcement, he wanted to gather his teammates, his coach, Mike Dunleavy, and Lakers owner Jerry Buss, to tell them his news, and we both knew that would be one of his toughest revelations. Sure enough, it was. I wasn't in the room for that private conversation, but I'll never forget the looks on the faces of those grown men—some of them crying, others ashen and shaking—when they walked out. It was such an incredibly sad moment; it took all I had to stare straight ahead and chant to myself, *Don't cry, Cookie. Whatever you do, don't cry.*

Cameras flashed all over the place as I, along with some of the Lakers coaches, a few of the players, and Earvin's doctor filed in and took our places in a row of seats near the podium. I sat directly behind the podium where, a moment later, my husband took his place. He leaned toward the microphone. "First of all, let me say good afternoon," Earvin said, clutching the edges of the podium. He cleared his throat. "Um, because of the HIV virus that I have attained," he said, "I will have to retire from the Lakers . . . today." A hush fell over the room, followed by a flurry of camera flashes. "I just want to make it clear that I do not have the AIDS disease, but the HIV virus." He paused and drew in a breath. "My wife is fine. She's negative. There's no problem with her. I plan on going on and living for a long time, so you'll see me around. Life will go on for me."

I don't think many people in that room or around the world believed my husband's life would go on for much longer. When I look back on it now, even I wasn't sure what the future would hold for us. The one thing I was sure of, though, was that the instant Earvin's diagnosis became public, my time on earth would be sharply divided into two halves: life before November 7, 1991, and life after that horrible day.

· *Our New Normal* ·

A lot of people have asked me whether I was angry with Earvin for contracting the HIV virus. We still have no idea how long he'd been carrying the virus by the time he was diagnosed, but we believe he got it from having unprotected sex with other women he'd been with during our twelve-year on-again, off-again relationship. Did I suspect that he'd been with many women and probably had plenty of unprotected sex? Yes. And while a long time would pass before I knew the full story of his lifestyle during those first few years with the Lakers—a time when we weren't even together—I didn't waste time on being upset with him. I'm not going to lie: the day he locked himself in a room to call each of his former sexual partners to tell them the news, it was awkward for me. But I didn't fret over it; he was calling women from his past. Besides, the truth of the matter is this: I couldn't focus on that part of it or waste energy being mad. I knew he wasn't running around trying to get sick on purpose or knowingly spreading the virus. Frankly, anger isn't the emotion you latch on to when

Anger isn't the emotion you latch on to when you're considering the mortality of the love of your life, anyway.

you're considering the mortality of the love of your life, anyway. After the initial shock, my sole focus was to figure out how to keep my husband from dying. Rather than stomp around the house demanding Earvin tell me the sordid details of his sexual past or waste time rooting for apologies, I read my Bible, asked my pastor in Toledo to pray for my husband, me, and our family, and then got down to the business of figuring out what he and I needed to do to keep him alive and have a healthy pregnancy.

On most days right after his diagnosis, I walked around like a zombie, as if I were technically alive but not really able to feel anything. It didn't help that I was pregnant, nauseous, and having trouble keeping anything down. Earvin did everything he could to support me, but I could see that he was balancing that while grasping for normalcy and trying to find his place in the world without basketball. Almost immediately after the announcement, the rumors popped up that he was either gay or bisexual; that had a lot to do with the widespread belief back then that AIDS was a gay person's disease. That whole period was so tough.

Even tougher: Earvin had suddenly gone from being at the height of his basketball career and very busy to sitting around the house. I could tell he was in pain, both physically and emotionally, and he slid into depression. He'd already formed the Magic Johnson Foundation—he did that soon after he'd met with Elizabeth Glaser, the AIDS activist—but he didn't do much else in the early days. He was still trying to wrap his head around the shock and devastation.

I dealt with the crisis the same way I'd always dealt with anything challenging: I studied the Bible and became more deeply involved in the church. And when I wasn't praying or praising, I was orchestrating Earvin's health plan and trying my best to reset our household to a new normal.

The first thing I did was take control of Earvin's diet. I hired a holistic chef, whose charge was to keep our refrigerator and plates stocked with fresh, organic whole foods. She pitched in with a few ideas of her own on what would help Earvin, including a steady cocktail of garlic. I appreciated her input, but we had to have a conversation about that stinky concoction of hers. "Look, I love my husband, and I want him to get healthy, but that garlic's got to go," I told her frankly one afternoon as she squeezed fresh garlic into a spoon for Earvin. I'd smelled it coming around the corner, and this then-pregnant lady, still in my first trimester, couldn't take it anymore.

Earvin immediately began taking AZT (zidovudine), the only medication that was available at the time to treat HIV. But it was hard for him to handle; it really upset his stomach. My husband has never been a complainer; he just does what he has to do. But AZT was pretty toxic and, though he didn't tell me he was nauseous or suffering from diarrhea, I noticed and knew it was taking its toll on him. Normally a sound sleeper who turned in early most nights, now Earvin was restless—incapable of getting a sound sleep. When he was awake, he'd spend inordinate amounts of time in the bathroom, nursing his upset stomach. Favorite foods he'd once loved, like collard greens, were no longer welcome on his plate; he couldn't keep them down. Like some kind of spy, I'd sneak and call the doctor and tell him, "I think you have to adjust his dosages; he's going to the bathroom a lot and he's getting weak," and the doctor would call later with a new directive for Earvin. I don't think Earvin was aware I was doing that. But it was important that I maintain that relationship with his team of doctors, whom

I trusted, as opposed to the whack jobs that were coming at us at NASCAR-level speeds. People started emailing and faxing their objections to his using AZT and making suggestions for their own drug cocktails, and when we were out, strangers would waltz right up to us with medical advice. One afternoon while we were having dinner at a restaurant in Beverly Hills, a man dressed in a long white robe and turban crowded our table and insisted on telling us about some antidote his "people" had discovered "back home."

"Yeah, I know you think I'm crazy, but it works," he insisted. "It's a process of stuff you have to do, but one of the things you have to do is drink your own urine . . ."

If only someone could have captured a photo of the look on our faces! We were expecting him to say something like, "You have to take this exotic herb from a rare tree in the mountains of Manassas" or something, but no: this man was standing over our dinner table, telling my husband he should drink human waste to get himself cured. "If you want to learn more, here's my number. Give us a call," he said, handing us his business card. Earvin and I looked at each other in shock, politely thanked the man for his advice, and went back to eating, trying hard to stifle our snickers. Later, when we got into the car, we both burst into laughter. "Now that's one we never heard before," Earvin said.

We were used to strangers approaching us, of course, but things had changed. Most people were polite, but I could tell some of them were afraid to come up to us; there weren't a lot of hugs or handshakes. I could understand why people were nervous, but it still hurt. The only ones we could count on to be unconditionally supportive were our family and close friends, for whom we were both grateful. If they were scared to touch us or be around us, they didn't really show it; they were too focused on giving us the loving care we needed to fill us up.

Soon enough, though, we decided to stop answering the phone and email, to talk only to our family and a select group of friends we could trust, and most important, focus on God. That was my plan—my goal: to make life for us as normal as possible. It was not lost on me that God had prepared me for this. Earvin was sure that God's purpose for him was to be the face of HIV so that he could help save people, but I was sure, too, that my purpose was to be right there by his side, to make sure that he could carry out God's mission. All along, God had been developing my faith, maturing it, and teaching me how to lean on it so that when we got to this place, we would be prepared, standing strong and sturdy as the biggest tree, our belief in Him so firmly rooted that not even this roaring, angry storm could knock us down. Every tool we needed to make it through, God had already put it in our hands.

My purpose was to be right there by his side, to make sure that he could carry out God's mission.

We did go to Hawaii the day after the announcement; we just needed a break. Another couple, some great friends who'd traveled with us before, went along. We thought that if we could get far enough away from the situation, we could forget about it for at least a time. But there was no escaping it. The paparazzi followed us everywhere, even to our quiet paradise away from the bright Los Angeles lights. Once while we were just sitting by the hotel pool, I noticed this long photo lens peeking through the bushes. Another time, as we made our way from the hotel to the house we'd rented, we saw a man getting into his car and pulling out of the parking lot at the same time as us. Suspicious, we made a series of turns to see if he was following us; sure enough, he was. Finally, we stopped, and our friends jumped out of the car like a SWAT team, banging on his windows.

"What are you doing?" they demanded. On his seat was a camera with a long, telescopic lens, much like the one I'd noticed peeking at us through the hotel bushes.

Scared, the paparazzo threatened to call the police. "I'll have you brought up on charges for harassment!" he yelled.

"Are you serious?" my friend said, equally loud. "You're the one creeping around the bushes!"

The whole world was talking about us and watching our every move. The only way we'd be able to relax, it seemed, was to leave the planet completely. At certain moments, I wished we could. Earvin was facing the same challenges as any other person who had HIV, but added to his trial was the pop cultural aspect of it all—the swirl of a celebrity at the height of his powers, dealing with a mysterious, deadly disease that the nation was, at the time, obsessed with, all while he and his pregnant wife tried to hold the media at bay. America was on a death watch, and the media was trying to get it all on film with zero regard for the fact that on the other side of their lenses were two human beings determined to beat the odds and desperate to do it without yielding to the titillation of the gossip obsessed.

It was a helluva pickle to be in as a mom-to-be, winding my way through my first trimester. This wasn't a part of the happy picture I'd colored when I dreamed of starting a family with Earvin. I thought I'd be planning for our baby—picking out colors for the nursery, buying little baby booties, thinking up names, and trying to figure out if the shape of my belly meant I was having a boy or a girl. Instead, I was nursing my husband through his illness and suffering a severe case of morning sickness that lasted around the clock, triggered by even the most mundane things: the smell of a potato chip, the sight of milk, the mere thought of standing next to someone who wasn't as fresh as humans should be when they're practicing good hygiene. One evening, when the housekeeper was whipping up a spaghetti and meat sauce dinner with extra garlic, I hid in our bedroom with the door shut tight and a towel smushed against the bottom of it, desperate to keep the scent from my nose. I wanted to tell her, "Go away, lady!" and I'm sure she thought I was either sad or I hated her because I wasn't being my usual kind self, but really, I was just sick. Another night, after eating an apple at Lon's house and getting in the car to go home, I begged Earvin to pull to the side of the road so that I could bring up that fruit, piece by piece. Eating a cracker, drinking ginger ale, sucking on peppermints—none of those things could tame my stomach. It was the worst.

It was in my mother's house that, finally, my stomach—and I—found peace. We'd traveled to Lansing and Detroit for Thanksgiving, a welcome respite from all the drama and a much-needed vacation with our families, whom we hadn't seen since Earvin's announcement. We'd talked on the phone, of course, and both our families had been so supportive; everything was, "We love you, we support you, what do you need?" But there was nothing like being home again.

· *There's No Place like Home* ·

I was born in Alabama, yes, but I spent my formative years in Detroit, where my family moved as part of the Great Migration, the wave of southern black families who trekked north in search of better jobs, housing, education, and respite from Jim Crow. I was only six when my parents crammed all of our things into the upper-level of a two-bedroom flat we shared with another family in Motor City and got down to the business of settling into the new black middle class. In Alabama, my father was cleaning offices, working as a tailor, and picking up as many odd jobs as he could get just to pay the rent and put food on the table. But when we left all that flat, green Alabama land and settled in the towering metropolis, home of Motown, capital of the automotive industry, abundance was finally tangible for Dad. It's where my father gained a financial foothold for his family. He got a job at Ford Motor Company and even went back to school to earn an education degree, while working that same job at Ford. For a short time, he even held down two jobs, working as a special education teacher in the daytime and then working nights at the automobile factory. But he never could make a transition into teaching full-time because it simply did not pay enough to keep a family of five afloat. Eventually, he gave up teaching altogether and focused solely on his factory gig, which paid well and provided the benefits our family needed.

The transition from Alabama to Detroit was not without its challenges. Those buildings were scary and imposing to a little girl whose height barely reached her mother's hip. Until then, I'd never seen anything like them and dreaded walking those five long blocks from our apartment to school, with the ring of honking cars in my ears and the smell of all that black factory smoke clouding the air, and those imposing buildings casting shadows, where, in Alabama, there was only sky and sunlight. The hardest part was dealing with our new neighbors, a rumble of mean street kids who made quick work of clowning my sister and me for being unapologetically southern. "Ooooh, y'all country!" they'd yell as we'd make our way home from school, sometimes running up to us and mushing our heads and pulling our hair as they poked fun or playing "smooch the booty," a game where the bigger boys would, literally, grab our behinds. Maybe they were right about us being "country": we didn't have fancy clothes, and a lot of times, Pat and I would take off our shoes and walk home barefoot because that was our way. Our southern twang didn't help matters. Pat didn't take any mess; she would protect me by shooing the boys away or threatening to pound them into the concrete. Still, dealing with their daily abuse and the grittiness of the city left us longing for a house—a home where we could ride our bikes and play with kinder friends and cocoon ourselves from the mean kids.

My father managed to save up enough to get us one, too, within about two years. I was in second grade when we moved into that place, a spacious house on a corner lot in a predominately white neighborhood. It had only two bedrooms and one bathroom, but the previous owners had converted the attic into bedrooms for the kids, and my father finished off the basement with a separate kitchen and space for a pool table, so really, compared to our apartment, it felt like a mansion. The day we moved in, people were standing on their porches, hands to their brows to shield the sun, just staring at us. No one said a word. For years, that's what it felt like—no one really talked to us, paid us much mind. I had one friend, a girl named Candace—she was the Candy to my Cookie—who loved for me to go over to her house to play, but only when her father wasn't home. Her mom was nice enough and her brother didn't pay me much mind, but the second she'd spot her father's car creeping up the road, it would be, "Hurry up, you gotta leave!" I accepted her at her word that her father just didn't like company at the house when he walked through his front door from a long day's work, but now, I know what was probably more true: he didn't want a black girl standing in his line of sight, in his living room.

I paid it little attention, though; everything I needed in terms of human connection I found in my own home. Because my father worked the late shift at the factory—he left for work in the afternoon while we were at school and wouldn't come back until well after midnight, when we were asleep—weekends were spent with him exploring the city. Pat was into her books, and my mother, well, she was busy cleaning and keeping everything in order, but I had no interest in sitting in the house learning typical "girl" things. My mother would yell out, "You need to stay here and let me teach you how to sew," and I would mumble to myself, *Yeah, hold that thought*, and then I'd yell out, "Dad! What are you and Harold doing today?" A bit of a tomboy, I wanted to be outdoors, exploring the city, so I would often tag along with my father and brother, who is two years my junior, when they went biking, or stumble on some fun at the ice or roller skating rink. Dad loved wrestling matches, so some Saturdays we'd find ourselves sitting front and center, watching two grown, sweaty men, grunting and roaring and tossing each other around a padded ring. When the roller derby made its way to Detroit, we became loyal Thunder Birds fans, getting to as many matches as money and time would allow. Then there were simpler pleasures: family dinners at McDonald's or Burger King, ice cream cones at Dairy Queen, birthday parties around the pool table in the basement. Family time was everything.

It didn't take long after we moved in for our neighborhood to shift demographics; after about two years of us living in that neighborhood, there were "For Sale" signs dotting lawns all the way down the street and well around the block, and soon enough, the black family on the other corner became the black family next door. That's when the community began to open its arms, when our house truly became a home. I'd be right there with the neighborhood kids, climbing trees, playing touch football, tag, and T-ball. My mother, who scored a job as a crossing guard to keep a little money of her own in her pockets, worked right on the corner where we lived and got to know all the children as she helped usher them on their daily ten-block walk to school. When she wasn't working or tending to the house, she was the mom on the block, keeping a watchful eye on us while we played, refereeing board games, swaying to the rhythm of the jump rope while we sang our double Dutch songs. I lived for when she'd hand out snacks or cold iced tea and water to us children. "Come on in and get some popsicles!" she would call out, stopping us in the throes of sweaty, sticky play in the thick heat of a summer's day. I couldn't help but smile watching her pass out those icy treats, happy that it was my mom who was providing that loving touch, that reminder that someone cared deeply both for us and our well-being.

That was the feeling I had standing in my mother's kitchen in Detroit that November after the world Earvin and I had fought so hard for came crashing down all around us: I felt safe. Like it was possible to pick up all the pieces and build something new. My mother opened her door, and I folded myself into her arms, grateful for the warmth of her breath on my ear as she whispered, "Everything is going to be all right."

My mother opened her door, and I folded myself into her arms, grateful for the warmth of her breath on my ear as she whispered, "Everything is going to be all right."

"Sit down, let me fix you a plate of chicken and dumplings," my mom said after she released me from her embrace.

Now, I have no idea what compelled my mother to serve chicken and dumplings; in my more than thirty years on the earth, she'd never made that dish for me. But there I was, at her kitchen table in Detroit, my home, sitting in front of this delectable stew, ready and able to inhale it like no other food I'd eaten—much less kept down—in my pregnancy. My body and the baby inside of it were responding to my mother's touch.

"Taste okay?" Mom asked, watching me eat.

"It's perfect."

It was. Everything. The food, our families, their uncon-ditional love, all of it, Earvin and I swallowed whole, happy to cocoon ourselves in that safe space. Our families knew we needed normalcy, and everyone was happy to give us the love and hugs we needed to fill us up. Traveling there was like taking the car to the filling station and pumping gas into an empty tank until that needle moved itself from "E" to "F." We could run again, and after that, our ride became a lot smoother.

I never got sick again after that bowl of chicken and dump-lings. Earvin and I were headed to our new normal.

Chapter Seven

A New Season

There are so many emotional benefits to the human touch. A caress of the arm, a warm hug, a pat on the back, a kiss on the cheek. Each of these everyday gestures, shared between lovers, friends, family, and even strangers represents the purest form of compassion—a fundamental acknowledgment of one's humanity. Humans need to be touched. Accepted. Loved.

Fear, resignation, and uneasiness made it hard for those who weren't sick to see—really see—past your sickness and down to your humanity. Your heart.

Sadly, that physical connection was, perhaps, one of the biggest personal casualties of going public with one's HIV status in the 1990s, when ignorance about the ways one contracted the virus ran high. Trusted information on the subject was scant. If you had HIV, hardly anyone wanted to touch you. Fear, resignation, and uneasiness made it hard for those who weren't sick to see—*really see*—past your sickness and down to your humanity. Your heart.

Maybe because he was a beloved celebrity, Earvin didn't have to face off against the everyday vitriol the average HIV-positive person did. During the question-and-answer part of his announcement, he asked the world to respect that he is a human being, with feelings, just like them: "All I want you guys to do is to give me a hug and ask me how I'm doing," he said simply. Interestingly, gratefully, people from around the world responded in kind; they'd come right up to us, offer their hands or open arms and say, "How are you?" Always, Earvin would say, "I'm doing just fine." It was the call-and-response of a superhero and his fans who, for the first time, were being forced to come to terms with the fact that Magic Johnson was magical on the court but human off it. Those exchanges were Earvin's air.

Still, announcing his status did hurt him in tangible ways: Pepsi and Nestlé pulled back on lucrative endorsement deals after he publicly disclosed, and, because people ignorantly thought HIV was a gay disease, rumors that my husband was bisexual were running rampant. We wouldn't find out until years later, either, that some of Earvin's family members were catching hell from friends, acquaintances, and coworkers who refused to touch, talk to, or otherwise be around them. What devastated my husband most, though, was being forced to give up what he loved more than anything in this world outside of God and his family: playing basketball. He was forced to bow out of the game because no one knew, yet, what the future held for him or the health risks he'd face playing at such a high level of intensity. His big announcement would be his farewell, minus the send-off we'd all imagined for him as he started thinking about retirement and how he'd say good-bye to the Lakers, the NBA, and the fans who'd cheered him on during the thirteen seasons he led his team. That depressed the hell out of Earvin.

> *What devastated my husband most, though, was being forced to give up what he loved more than anything in this world outside of God and his family: playing basketball.*

It was heartbreaking to see the life seeping out of my husband—to watch him lying around the house, bored, miserable, and dejected. He'd already set up the Magic Johnson Foundation and was pouring some of his energy into getting it on its feet, but really, when it was all said and done, in the time it took for him to finish a press conference, he'd reduced himself to a sick, unemployed basketball player who would spend the rest of his days being an outcast—a footnote in his own legacy.

I understood his sadness, but I didn't want to cohost that pity party. I needed Earvin focused on our future together. I needed him—for his sake, for my sake, for the sake of our baby—to put one foot in front of the other and move forward. So I became that bee, constantly buzzing in his ear. If I saw him lying around, I'd plop down right next to him and crank up the conversation: "So, what are we going to do for vacation?" or "What would you like for dinner tonight?" Some days, I'd overwhelm him with baby planning: "What do you think about yellow and brown for the nursery?" and "Can you help me come up with a list for the baby shower registry?" and "When the baby comes, you think maybe we should skip hiring a nurse?" Many days, I'd encourage him to get dressed and head out to a game, knowing that just being in the stadium, cheering on his team, breathing in the energy of the game, coaches, and players would, even if only for a couple hours, pump some happiness into his veins.

Ultimately, it was the fans who made Earvin whole again. When they voted him into the All-Star game, NBA commissioner David Stern agreed to let him play. I was excited for him because playing in the game would give him a chance to compete one more time. But I was worried, too, because I didn't know how the people who voted him in would react to him being on the court—whether they would cheer or boo him—or if his fellow athletes would have a problem playing against him. This was certainly on Earvin's mind. As he was preparing to play in the All-Star game, I knew something was affecting him—that something was off. Earvin was a nervous wreck—pacing the floor in the hotel room, fiddling and twitching with the newspapers on the coffee table, so distracted that he barely noticed life going on all around him. He didn't have his game face on; warrior mode had been replaced by an anxiousness I hadn't seen before. I sat next to him on the couch and absentmindedly rubbed my growing belly. "Are you okay?" I asked, hoping to ease the tension.

Earvin clasped his hands and looked down, quiet for a moment. "Yeah," he said. "I'm just a little nervous."

I gently touched his chin, turned his face toward mine, and kissed him. "You just go out there and be Earvin. Do your thing like you always did. Don't worry about anybody else, just play hard and have a good time." With that, I gave him the biggest hug, and, in my embrace, I could feel his body loosen, the tension easing its way out. "You got this."

Earvin got on that court and showed out. He finished that game with twenty-five points, nine assists, and the MVP trophy hoisted in the air. What's more, the voices of players who thought the earth would stop spinning if an HIV-infected person played in the game were completely drowned out by Earvin's Magic Show on the court, plus the willingness of Detroit forward Dennis Rodman and Philadelphia power forward Charles Barkley to square up against him, hip to hip, chest to chest, sweat against sweat, completely dispelling the notion that fear should factor into playing Magic hard in the paint. I don't think I've ever cheered louder than when I saw those physical exchanges; I knew what it meant to Earvin. What it meant to me. Being voted into the All-Star game by the fans was one thing, but suiting up for it, playing at that level of intensity, having the unyielding support of respected competitors in the league, and riding back to our home with that trophy in his lap was just the medicine we both needed to make saying good-bye to the game a little more palatable. It also reintroduced my husband to his confidence and sent a clear message to everyone watching that HIV wasn't going to stop Earvin; he had, and still has, plenty of life in him. Plenty of fight.

That muscle he needed to soldier on only grew stronger when Commissioner Stern gave Earvin another vote of confidence, allowing him to stay on the 1992 Summer Olympic "Dream Team" roster, alongside stars including Michael Jordan, Larry Bird, and Charles Barkley. It could have been just as easy for Stern to yield to the hushed demands of the likes of players like Karl Malone, who wanted Earvin banned, but the commissioner's approval sent a powerful message of tolerance that crossed continents. Not only would my husband become the face of the heterosexual HIV community and give hope to so many others living with the virus, Earvin would have a platform to show the world that the stigma attached to an HIV diagnosis was plain dumb.

On a more personal level, it was superstars Michael Jordan, Larry Bird, and Charles Barkley who got Earvin feeling normal again. During the national exhibition season leading up to the Olympic games in Barcelona, Spain, the three of them would make it clear not just in word but deed that Earvin was still one of the guys. They'd joke with him, pick at him, drag him out of his hotel room for dinner, or just to hang out. Michael, in particular, took him in like a brother, and when I witnessed the two of them together, I would get teary watching them laugh and joke and be normal. Around them, Earvin's sickness was irrelevant; it didn't exist. It was just him, basketball, and the fellas again. It was the best thing anybody could have ever done for him, and for that, I'm so grateful.

Though he attempted a comeback in the 1992–1993 season, Earvin could not overcome the scrutiny of his peers to make it back to the court. While he was practicing with his team and participating in exhibition games, there were grumblings from around the league about the risk of guarding a man with HIV. Men— friends—with whom Earvin had played for years suddenly backed away from him when he suited up for practice and ran drills, afraid his sweat or blood from battle scars hard won in sometimes brutal NBA competitions would make them vulnerable to the virus. It didn't matter that the odds of them becoming infected in that scenario were about as likely as one of them getting simultaneously struck by both a bus and by lightning; emotions made statistics and logic irrelevant to players who believed deep down in their gut that even running up the same court as my husband would be equivalent to a death sentence. Players like Karl Malone were actively and publicly campaigning to have my husband banned from the league altogether out of fear that they would "catch" AIDS from guarding him. That hurt Earvin. It hurt me and our family. And ultimately, Earvin decided not to return to the game that season.

He did coach for a short while, and then went back to playing for half a season in 1996, but ultimately decided that the game was no longer for him. Still, life wasn't over for him—not even by a stretch. God had a much bigger purpose in mind.

· *A New Normal* ·

When Earvin was still playing exhibition games as part of the Olympics team, life was finally starting to feel normal again; I spent my time keeping our house running, planning for the baby, and settling into being upbeat and positive, not just for my husband but also for our growing family. Still, there were times when darkness would overshadow the light I tried to walk in as our child's birth grew near. I didn't have HIV and everyone knew this, but that didn't really shield me from the stigma and scrutiny that came with being married to a man who did, even, I suspected, within the medical establishment itself. An exchange with my obstetrician left me wondering whether a medical procedure he insisted I submit to was being ordered out of fear rather than logic.

"Would you like to have an amniocentesis?" my doctor asked, referring to the invasive procedure that helps doctors determine whether a developing fetus has chromosomal abnormalities or infections. The test, which requires a doctor to insert a needle into the amniotic sac to draw out fluid, carries a small risk of miscarriage.

"No," I answered casually. "I'm only thirty-two and everything I've read says it's not necessary to have one unless you're pregnant after age thirty-five."

The doctor stared at me, his eyes pensive. "You're right, we usually do it for patients at age thirty-five or older, but we want to make sure that you and the baby are okay," he said. "We strongly suggest you have it."

"I don't understand why," I said, rubbing my stomach, now slightly alarmed by the insistence. "Is there something wrong with the baby?"

"Not that we can see at all," the doctor assured me. "Everything seems perfectly normal."

"Okay, so why would I need to have one?"

My obstetrician pushed a little harder, reiterating my age and all the different disorders my child could be born with. I insisted I didn't want to take the risk and made clear that, no matter if my child was revealed to have abnormalities, I would keep him and love him strong. He finally dropped the amnio discussion. Still, even after I made my objections clear, a few days later, Lon's wife, Laurie, called to convince me to change my mind. Because I'd never told her about my private, intimate meetings with my doctor, I can only assume that someone in the office recruited Laurie, who shared the same doctor, as an emissary. She was unapologetic and relentless. "Cookie, I understand that you made the decision not to have the test, but I think you really should do it so you know for sure everything is okay with the baby," she said. "Don't you want to know what's going on? The appointment is tomorrow. I really think you need to be there."

I was taken aback, and certainly upset that she was inserting herself into my health decisions. What's worse: Earvin was out of town commentating games, so I couldn't get in touch with him to get his opinion or support in the matter. With the doctor practically demanding I have the amnio and Laurie in my ear, I caved. I was scared, but I went through with it. What made the test even more harrowing was that it came just as things were starting to calm down; finally, Earvin and I were settling into our new way of life after his diagnosis, and now I had to go through another excruciating period of not knowing if the baby was harmed by the test or if he was HIV-positive. It took a lot of prayer and meditation on God's word to give me the peace to get through that part.

I don't know why the doctor was so insistent; maybe he really was concerned about my age, or maybe he was worried about my baby's HIV status. I'm just not sure, though it is something I've always wondered about. Thank God, the baby was not hurt by that test and that it confirmed what we already knew: the baby was not HIV-positive. That one experience with my ob-gyn notwithstanding, he was a fantastic doctor, and I happily stuck with him through my entire pregnancy and delivery. After that situation, I took my pregnancy in stride and settled into enjoying it.

That joy was doubled when my sister, Pat, whom I'd asked to stand in as my partner in birth classes, went above and beyond

Cookie Kelly at six months old.

Barbizon modeling shot of Cookie at age fourteen.

Cookie's first job at the Madison Movie Theater as a junior in high school.

Adrianne and Cookie freshman year in their dorm room at Michigan State University.

Earvin and Cookie share a kiss at Michigan State University.

Earvin, Cookie, and Ron Charles (Penny's boyfriend and Earvin's teammate).

Mark Aguirre, Earvin, Cookie, Jackie Hubbard, Isiah and Lynn Thomas, and Angie Aguirre.

Cookie graduates Michigan State University, December 1981.

Cookie and Earvin on a trip to the Bahamas, summer of 1984.

Andre, at age ten, and Earvin in Los Angeles.

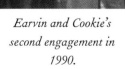

Earvin and Cookie's second engagement in 1990.

Adrienne, Cookie, and Anita Scott (right) at the 1991 NBA Finals in Chicago.

Earl Kelly walking his daughter Cookie down the aisle, September 14, 1991, in Lansing, Michigan.

Married! Cookie and Earvin at their wedding reception at Kellogg Center on the Michigan State University campus.

Michael Stennis, Earvin, and Cookie in Hawaii days after Earvin's 1991 announcement.

Earvin Jr. receiving the 1992 NBA All-Star MVP award, with Earvin Sr., Cookie (pregnant with EJ), and Mom Johnson in Orlando.

Pat and Cookie (pregnant) heading out to a wedding in 1992.

Cookie opening gifts at her baby shower in May 1992 in Los Angeles.

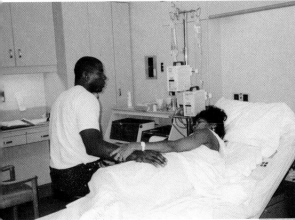

Earvin comforting Cookie in labor June 1992 in Los Angeles.

Earvin holding Earvin Johnson III just after birth in June 1992.

Cookie and Earvin (with his medal) holding EJ at the 1992 Olympics in Barcelona, Spain.

Cookie with a young EJ and baby Elisa on Christmas Eve 1994 when Elisa was delivered to the Johnsons.

Young EJ and Earvin on their basketball court in Beverly Hills, 1994.

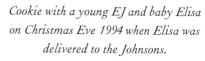

Baby shower for Elisa with Eula, Sharon, Gina, Cookie (holding Elisa), Glynis, Sheri, and Page in 1995.

Cookie, presiding judge, Earvin (holding Elisa), and EJ at Elisa's adoption during the summer of 1995 in Los Angeles.

Hawaii family vacation with Andre, Earvin, EJ, Cookie, and Elisa in 1995.

Andre, Earvin, Cookie, Elisa, and EJ at Earvin and Cookie's 10th anniversary celebration in 2001.

EJ and Cookie at a school event in Los Angeles.

Cookie and Elisa at Elisa's high school baccalaureate service in 2013 in Los Angeles.

Cookie in the CJ by Cookie design room in January 2013 in Los Angeles.

Earvin and Cookie enjoying vacation on a yacht in Sorrento, Italy, in July 2015.

Earvin and Cookie at Cookie's 40th birthday party in Los Angeles.

the request and put in for a transfer from her Air Force job in San Antonio to a different gig in Los Angeles and moved close by. It was the sweetest thing she could have done; honestly, I thought she would catch a flight to LA a few times, rush over to my classes, and hold my hand and let me lean on her while I practiced my breathing techniques. But I hadn't expected, even for a minute, that she would uproot her entire life to resettle close by and volunteer to be my rock. We didn't have the easiest relationship growing up; we were two different people with distinct personalities, likes, and needs. She liked staying in the house and reading, and I loved ripping and running outdoors; she was reserved and quiet, I was a bit more outgoing. But when Pat arrived on the scene, our relationship moved to a different level of understanding and camaraderie that not only filled my heart but also put me at ease. Simply put: Pat was there for me, and with her around, I felt safe, protected. There never was a doubt in my mind that she had my back.

There was no better proof of this than when my sister drove me through the smoldering streets of Los Angeles two days after the 1992 Rodney King riots began. It was such a scary, harrowing time; the entire city, it seemed, was on fire, and we were witnessing it all unfold from our backyard, which overlooks the neighborhood that was the center of the unrest. By the time the six-day siege was over, fifty-three people had lost their lives, more than two thousand were injured, and the marines and National Guard were wrestling order in the middle of $1 billion in property damages. As luck would have it, the day after the riots, one of my two crazy cocker spaniels, Freddie, swan-dived over the back ledge of our yard and landed just beyond a tree, out of reach from our rescue. Only Earvin, with his long, lean body and massive hands, had the physicality to jump down into the brush, scoop up the dog, and then foist himself back up the ledge to safety. Poor Freddie's life had been spared, but he was seriously injured. "You need to bring him in," the doctor said after I frantically explained Freddie's condition. The vet thought Freddie might have broken at least one leg.

Problem was the vet was in the center of the neighborhood where the riots took place. Indeed, it seemed the only building left standing was the vet's office. But Pat bravely hustled me into her car, strapped my pregnant self in the front with Freddie on my lap, and drove right into the center of the chaos. Even with the windows rolled up, the smell of the smoke singed our noses; police and members of the military were on every corner and every block in between, and the restlessness of both them and the people who lived there was palpable. I was anxious and desperate to get off the streets and into the vet's office, but we had to creep through. When Pat stopped at a light, a group of bystanders, intense and pensive, peered into our car, and started screaming: "That's Cookie! Hey—that's Cookie Johnson!" I nearly lost it, but Pat kept her cool, easily navigating her car from the light and to the vet's office, where she watched over me while I tended to Freddie. I'll never forget how protected and loved I felt with her by my side; that same feeling remains, all these years later. From that moment, our bond as sisters became boundless and, to this day, she is my closest confidante, counselor, supporter, and friend.

When he could, Earvin spoiled me rotten, too. When he wasn't traveling, he was home, right by my side, following me around the house, babying me, and making sure that I was protected. I'd reach for a bowl on the second tier of shelves in the kitchen, and he would rush in and grab it for me with a sweet warning and a kiss on the cheek: "Be careful with all that reaching. You don't want to hurt the baby." Beyond that, he spent all of his free time with me, talking, laughing, enjoying my company, and opening up every part of himself to me, even what was going on with his career and the fallout from his HIV disclosure. This was a big deal because it was new; up until then, that kind of one-on-one time was rare, as was that level of detail and discussion about his business affairs. Our relationship, it seemed, elevated from two people dating and in love to husband and wife, in this life together. Just like I was there for Earvin, he was there for me, even down to the constant baby chatter. He didn't bristle when I talked about baby showers and registries, or fabrics for the glider, or artwork for the baby's room. He was right there with me—a rare thing for a professional athlete, for sure. Most times, you're lucky if he makes it to the birth.

I made sure Earvin made it to our baby's birth, though. By May of that year, I was in my last trimester and biding my time until my due day, June 14, when my doctor told me my baby was ready to pop. "You're starting to dilate already," he said, as I sat up from the table and adjusted my examination robe. "You could have this baby as early as next week if you want to."

"What do you mean?" I asked.

"Well, you're two weeks out, so technically, your baby could be born today and be healthy," my doctor offered. "If you want to plan the birth, I'm happy to arrange it on whatever day you choose. I'll induce you, and he'll be here when you want him to be here."

My doctor didn't have to say that twice. I jumped at the chance to plan our son's birthday, knowing it would make it more likely that Earvin could be in town to be by my side as our son took his first breath. To this day, my mother still makes fun of me for it. After that doctor's appointment, I went home and immediately started combing over Earvin's calendar, searching for a date within the next two weeks when he would have a small window to fly home. As it turned out, Earvin was scheduled that next week to be in Chicago on one day, then take a day-long break, and then fly out to Portland for another exhibition game. The day of that break was June 4—a most perfect day to meet our son.

So the morning of June 4, my sister, Pat, drove me to the hospital for the delivery. I was excited, scared. Ready. My doctor administered the Pitocin, a synthetic hormone that makes the uterus contract, and by noon, just as I was going into labor, Earvin walked in, right on time. Pat was at the foot of the bed, documenting the delivery of her nephew on camera (an experience that, for her, was so harrowing to watch, she vowed never to have kids and had her tubes tied two weeks later). After eight hours of pushing, our son Earvin Johnson III, was born, a joy we'd never known. His birth also ushered in the greatest fear I'd never known. From the moment the doctor grabbed him and ushered him to the side of my bed to clean him up, I literally held my breath, waiting desperately to hear that my child was healthy—that he was affected neither by the virus nor the stress that racked my body while I carried him to term. But EJ didn't cry. Even after the doctor popped his bottom, our son made not one peep. The doctor went to work, rubbing him down and clearing his passageways, then popped EJ again; this time, he wailed. Still holding my breath, I listened as the doctor gave us the good news: "He's fine, beautiful, and healthy. Nothing is wrong with him."

And with those words, I finally let go and breathed, pushing out a deep, powerful exhale and a rebel cry that made Earvin jump. "Cookie!" he admonished, shocked by my loud sobs. "All that crying! What are you crying about?"

When I think about it today, I realize that my scream was a sigh of relief from the worry I'd held during practically my entire pregnancy. Though the doctors had said early on that our baby was not HIV-positive, there was still a part of me that was afraid that something would be wrong with him—that he would be harmed in some way. When he didn't cry immediately, I thought my worst fear was about to be realized. I needed to hear my child's little voice and the doctor's pronunciation to know that everything would be okay—to know that it was okay to breathe. To this day, Earvin makes fun of me for the outburst; he thinks it's hysterical.

Honestly, what was funnier to me was that the doctors thought EJ had jaundice because his skin was yellow. There wasn't anything wrong with the boy; he was just a yellow black baby. We could tell by looking at his fingers and the tips of his ears that he would get browner, but the doctor insisted on keeping him a few days and giving him light therapy to make sure he wasn't jaundiced. I stayed in the hospital, too, to be with our son and also to get a few days extra rest before we hopped into the whirlwind of new parenting.

Little did I know, though, that the drama of new motherhood would meet me at the door of our home—literally. Unbeknownst to me, Earvin planned a "welcome home" party for the baby and me, and had a basement full of our closest friends waiting at the house when we arrived. This, of course, freaked out my mom, who was convinced that newborns should be handled only by their parents and close caregivers in the first weeks, lest they contract germs and diseases from excessive contact with the general public. Convinced the party guests would kill the baby, my mother headed off contact at the pass: she met Earvin, the baby, and me at the front door, snatched EJ, and took off running up the stairs.

"Mom, what are you doing?" I asked, calling after her, exasperated.

"They're going to breathe on him and put germs on him," she yelled back angrily. "You two can't raise this baby. You don't know what you're doing!"

Earvin, unmoved, went down to the basement to greet the guests while I went upstairs to calm my mother and get myself presentable for our guests. Once we were settled, I took the baby to see our company, my mother fast on our heels, repeatedly warning everyone, "Don't touch him!" Her tolerance threshold was about five minutes; after that, she again snatched EJ and ran back upstairs to save him from the germs.

I had bigger concerns than who was touching my baby, though. In the first two days, I couldn't get EJ to eat. With the help of a lactation specialist, I'd managed to breastfeed him while in the hospital, but when I got home, he wouldn't latch on to feed. In fact, I couldn't even get him to open his little mouth. I would offer my breast and he would turn away and defiantly purse his lips. Of course, in my mind, this meant he was going to starve to death. "I'm a terrible mother," I cried as I sought advice from some of my girlfriends. "What am I going to do?"

"Take your time," they told me. "When he's hungry, he will eat."

An entire day passed without EJ eating; after the second day, I freaked out and called the hospital. They sent a lactation nurse, who gave me a no-nonsense approach to getting my child to eat.

"Take his little head, smash it on the nipple so that he can't breathe," she said. "When he can't breathe, he'll open his mouth. That's when you shove your breast in there. He will eat."

I looked on, horrified, as she grabbed my breast and used it to practically smother my son. My sister, Pat, had to hold back my mom, who, like me, thought that, surely, the tactic would kill poor little EJ. But it didn't; sure enough, he opened his mouth and suckled, getting his fill. Though the entire experience was traumatic, after a second lactation visit, both he and I were pros, and I couldn't feed that kid enough. Every two hours, like clock-work, he breastfed like a champion.

While I was busy getting used to being a mom and settling into EJ's routine, Earvin was preparing to head to Barcelona for the Olympics, on an international basketball high that has yet to be matched. He was going as part of the Dream Team, the first Olympic roster of U.S. players to include professional ath-letes. The team was an international cultural phenomenon, and Michael, Larry, Charles, and, yes, Earvin were being feted like rock stars in Spain and in media throughout the world. It was an exciting time because the prowess of our most beloved American players was helping the sport explode on an international stage. My husband was an enthusiastic ambassador who, after such an incredible low just seven months before, was riding high on the glory he and his friends were receiving for doing what they loved. On a more personal level, Earvin was focused on performing at the height of his powers because he was convinced this series would be his final hurrah as a professional basketball player.

In my new mom haze, I'd totally forgotten that Earvin was leaving until I saw him packing his suitcase.

"Wait!" I exclaimed. "You have to leave, don't you?"

"Yes," he said matter-of-factly as he carefully folded and organized his clothes. "I'm going to Portland for a few days, and then we're flying out to Barcelona."

Stunned, I sat and watched him finish packing his suitcase and haul it down to the front door, where his father, who'd come with his mother to visit and help with the baby, waited to help Earvin load the car. By the time they got the suitcases in the trunk, I burst into tears. "No!" I exclaimed. "Please don't leave me! You can't leave us now! We need you!"

Earvin's dad pulled me close and reassured me that everything would be okay. "Come here, baby," he said, hugging me. "I got you. Everything is going to be okay."

Earvin kissed me and piled on some reassurances of his own. "Don't worry, Cookie. I'll see you in a couple weeks. Maybe you and the baby can come to Barcelona to see the games."

"Really?" I asked.

"Sure," he said. "I would love that."

Not wanting to miss out on the chance to support my husband's proverbial victory lap, I made the decision to pack up our newborn son and head to Spain two weeks after Earvin left. I wanted to support him in person. Of course, I had a chorus of naysayers in my ear, protesting my decision and suggesting I needed my head checked. Who, after all, takes a newborn on a trip across the other side of the world to see a basketball game? But I wanted to be there. Playing in this game meant the world to Earvin, and I wanted to be front and center as he took his last bow. I also wanted to witness the history being made when the Dream Team took the court. The whole world, it seemed, was watching to see what this team of superstars would do, and I was excited to be a part of it.

Now, getting to Spain with a newborn was certainly tricky. I had to get the baby a passport, as he couldn't travel internationally without one, even if he was barely a month old. I had to fill out papers and hand over a little picture of our tiny baby and everything. Because it was paramount that I protect little EJ from deadly germs that could attack his still-developing immune system, I had to find a way to minimize public interaction and assure that we'd travel in transportation that was super clean and accommodating. Luckily, Lon was able to get me a seat on MGM Grand, a now-defunct airline that operated opulent, all-first-class flights with limited seating and a private terminal. I flew from Los Angeles to New York on MGM, and then continued to Barcelona with the crew. Earvin's mother, Christine, came along with me to keep watch over the baby while I went to the games and, well, also to help me get used to handling a newborn. I was, after all, a novice—a new mom, juggling a new baby, in a foreign country. But we made it work. Had to. I knew for sure that it was worth it when our car pulled up in front of the hotel and Earvin ran out of the hotel to greet us, his arms outstretched to hug me, his mom, and especially his baby, whom he'd sorely missed after going two weeks without seeing his little face. "I'm so glad you're here," he said, smiling. In that moment, we were one.

We were, and forever will be, despite the odds, through goodness, sickness, and health, the Johnson Family. Love was, and remains, the place to be.

Chapter Eight

EJ's Freedom

It was the swirls in my mother's skirt that fascinated him—the colors, the movement, the snap of the fabric as it danced against her skin and the breeze it created as she whirled. "Twirl, Grandy!" EJ would demand, clapping and giggling and spinning right beside her. "Twirl, twirl, twirl!" He was about three years old, the perfect age to be fascinated by such things during playtime with his grandmother. He was super active then, just like most kids at that age—quick to jump and kick and swing on the monkey bars and dance and run with the wind. But it was the colors, the fabric, and the grandeur of the swish that moved him.

I thought EJ's fascination was rooted in his newfound ability to see the colors and the movement. An undiagnosed stigmatism had grossly affected his ability to see until age three, and when he finally got his glasses, a whole new world opened up to him. Thus, EJ's fascination with twirling and colors and pretty things. That, at least, was my prevailing wisdom on the matter. That was my thinking, too, when I considered EJ's penchant for playing dress-up at preschool during free play. Every afternoon, the teachers would lead the children over to a box in a colorful area of the huge playroom and encourage them to dig through the costumes in search of something that would spark their imagination and role-playing. Inevitably, EJ gravitated straight to anything Disney princess: Snow White, Cinderella, Belle from *Beauty and the Beast*, and all the others. Disney princesses wore colorful, fancy dresses he could climb into and spin around in just like his grandmother did—much more visually interesting, for sure, than the play construction hat and stiff work overalls, or any of the other dress-up costumes that the boys tended to choose. "Watch me!" he'd say, laughing as he swished the dramatic dresses to and fro. Truly, I thought nothing more of his love for long skirts and dramatic dresses than that because, well, EJ was a baby, developmentally on track with other little three-year-olds who, at that age, seemed to thrive on using their imaginations. A simple cardboard box in their hands could transform into spaceships perfect for fantastic voyages; belts were just the right lassos to turn brooms into a herd of wild horses they could ride. If he

His happiness made my heart full.

wanted to twirl in a dress like his Grandy, I had not one problem with it. It made him happy. And his happiness made my heart full.

Still, EJ's fondness for princess dresses raised a few eyebrows—enough so that one afternoon, one of the teachers called a quick side conference with me. "Do you know that he's going over there putting on skirts?" she asked in a hushed tone.

"Well," I said, hesitantly, meeting her inference with a mother's rationale, "when we're home, you know, we dance, and my mom has skirts and maybe he's attracted to it because he wants to mimic what she does."

"No," she said, shaking her head. "He's putting on the little shoes and pretending to be Cinderella and Snow White. It's fine. There's nothing wrong with it. I just thought you should know."

When he was still doing it at age five, the teachers were tapping me on my shoulder a little harder as my son continued to dress up in the princess outfits and started reaching for baby dolls to dress, feed, and nurture at playtime and other "typically girl" toys. My thoughts about his behavior evolved, along with my approach to guiding my son's interests. "He's creative," I reasoned to the teachers and friends I'd checked in with to gauge whether I should be concerned. "He thinks with the left side of his brain. Maybe he doesn't like trucks because he can use his imagination a little better with the kitchen sets and the doll babies. He'll grow out of it."

Frankly, I wasn't sure of any of this. All I knew was that I was becoming increasingly concerned about the chatter surrounding my son, the subtle policing of his behavior, and, if I'm honest about it, what his actions said about him—about how he would fit in with society's ideas of what little boys are truly made of, particularly since he was the son of Magic Johnson, American superhero. That came with a catalogue of expectations: that the son of one of the best American athletes of our generation would be athletic, maybe play basketball or football, run track, chase women, be an alpha male. Instead, my son, overweight, bespectacled, wanted to dress up like a girl.

So I went on the offensive, starting with telling my baby what he could and couldn't do. "You're a boy," I would tell him ever so gently. "You have to play with boy things." And then I parachuted EJ into the center of a boy's world: Tonka trucks, toy trains, Batman costumes, touch football, and T-ball.

What is that saying about the "best-laid plans"? Let's just say mine backfired.

EJ was no more interested in catching that football, chasing his opponents down the field, hitting that stupid T-ball, and running around those bases than he was taking a heaping tablespoon of castor oil: none of it appealed. In his T-ball games, all the other kids would wait around the bases, yelling, "Hit the ball to me!" and my son would be in the outfield picking flowers. "Look, Mommy! Look at the yellow in this one!" he'd be yelling.

I'd just shake my head and say, "Oh, Lawd," exasperated. "They're really pretty, honey, but look for the ball!"

By the time he was up at bat, he'd have a whole bouquet in his fist. "These are for you, Mommy," he'd say so sweetly as he pushed them toward me.

Granted, T-ball was a challenge for him; he was still working through his prior vision issues, which had led to problems with his motor skills and body awareness, so seeing, hitting, catching, and chasing after the ball were tough enough. Adding in a lack of interest made that sport pretty much dead in the water for my child. His experience out on the football field was even worse: everyone would be running down the field, and EJ would still be standing there. "Run, EJ!" Earvin and I would yell. "Go get the ball!" While his teammates traversed the field, their feet carrying them as fast as the wind, EJ would get as stiff as a statue and just stand there.

After that season, Earvin put his foot down: "That's it, no more sports for him. Leave him alone. This is not his thing."

I'm not going to lie: that pronouncement, that decision seared. I'd often imagined, after all, that with Earvin's DNA coursing through his veins and my athleticism running in his blood, EJ would, at the very least, be athletic. I'd often imagined Earvin and EJ out in the backyard tossing the football around and challenging each other on the basketball court, with my husband schooling our son on what it takes to be a star athlete like him. That part didn't happen often; though he was no longer playing, Earvin was still deep into the intense NBA travel schedule, this time as a commentator, plus busy building his post–professional basketball empire. He made very little time for casual play. "But it's too early to say he's not into sports," I'd argue. "If you would just take him outside and throw a ball with him, teach him some of your skills, he could get it. Just try. He can learn it."

But Earvin knew. Game recognizes game. Even at the youngest of age—he was about ten, to be precise—Earvin knew he had this thing within that made him an extraordinary athlete. And because he'd been around athletes all his life, he could tell the makings of an athlete versus a kid who didn't have the skills. To him, it was simple: "Look," he said. "It's obvious sports isn't his thing. Just look! Leave him alone and let him do what he wants to do."

Deep down, though, I was concerned and afraid of what EJ really wanted to do. In addition to helping to manage his weight, getting EJ to focus on sports was supposed to distract him from his desire to do all those "girly" things, and now, even that was off the table. I was stumped.

And then it hit me: I needed to focus not so much on appearances and what others thought about my son, but on EJ's happiness—on what made him put in his all. In that respect, Earvin was right: I needed to let our son do what appealed to him and his natural abilities—something that inspired and, at the same time, addressed his most critical needs.

This much I was sure of: EJ loved music, colors, and clothing. He also needed to get some of that weight off him and, after a diagnosis with attention deficit disorder, a way to engage with a creative way of learning, particularly when it came to reading. It wasn't long before I came up with the perfect appeal: I enrolled EJ in the Youth Academy of Dramatic Arts, an after-school and weekend theater program.

It was perfect. There, he had to learn how to read and memorize lines, which helped increase his engagement with words and focus his attention on a specific goal. Plus, my baby was happy. Finally. Acting opened a door that had been inaccessible to him because we were trying to get him to do "boy" things. EJ blossomed. By the time he was seven, he had his first major role, as the maniacal dentist in a stage production of *Little Shop of Horrors*. He had a long white coat—no he didn't twirl in it, but he did enjoy wearing it—and put his all into the lines, to the applause of his parents and the audience. No doubt, he loved theater because he could act and pretend to be something different, without the judgment and ridicule that came when he refused to restrict himself inside the rigid gender boxes he'd come to recognize in his short time on this planet. By then, he was well aware of others' expectations for boys—what the stakes were. Some of that came at school from a few of the other kids, but EJ wasn't safe from that kind of thinking even at home. I was still rooting for him to play like and with boys, and I tried everything to force the issue, even curating a monthly all-boy playgroup with some of my friends. He had no problem playing with them the way that they chose to play, but mostly he requested playdates with girls, where he could sit in their rooms and play with dolls.

At home, I did my best to drastically limit his access to traditional dolls. I avoided buying baby dolls designed specifically for girls, allowing him to play only with stuffed animals that were identifiable as "boy" toys. My compromise was to purchase those that he could dress up. One special stuffed animal he loved in particular was Clifford the Big Red Dog, fashioned after the main character in the hit children's TV show and book series. Someone had given it to him as a present. EJ loved Clifford because it came with a couple of little vests that he could use to dress up the stuffed animal. I loved it because Clifford offered the best of both worlds: he was a neutral toy, which hid the nature of my son's play, but also allowed him to play with it in the way that he wanted to because Clifford came with clothes. I even purchased a few additional outfits for Clifford so that EJ would have wardrobe options for his new favorite toy. In this way, Clifford met both of our needs. EJ could take it to his friends' houses, without raising eyebrows or incurring judgment, which, in turn, made me more comfortable.

It was Oprah, though, who put me on the path to a breakthrough with the way I came to accept my son's fluid gender identity. She was the Bible back then; if she said it was a thing, it was a thing, and if she said there was a cure, well, you put in a rush order to get some of that medicine in your system. One particular episode of *Oprah* focused on gender identity and the crises it caused in families who were grasping with the very things I was dealing with in my own home. Featured were kids who identified as transgender, despite that their families refused to acknowledge them as such. One woman tearfully recounted the story of her son, who had long told his family that he was, indeed, a girl, only to be rebuffed by his parents and all those who loved him. The child was eight at the time of the interview; a psychologist very calmly told his mother that there was nothing she could do to change him, because she'd waited too late to seek help to modify his desires and behavior. Had she sought professional help when the boy started displaying signs of wanting to switch gender identity at, say, age two or three, "you might have been able to stop this," he said.

Hearing him say that made me burst into tears. EJ was seven at the time, and I'd known from when he was age two or three that he more strongly identified with girls, but I never sought out help. And here was this man on *Oprah*, telling me that this was my fault—that had I done my job as a mother and simply gotten a professional involved, all the grief, all the confusion, all the hiding, all the pleading, all the worrying and pushing, would have long ago come to an end. I felt absolutely horrible—as if I'd failed my son and my responsibilities as a parent.

Then came Oprah's interview with the boy. Through tears, I watched as he sat on her sofa, dressed in a skirt and blouse, telling his mother matter-of-factly, "I don't understand why you're upset about this. This is who I am. Can't you see that I'm a girl?" He'd been telling his mother from the moment he could form words in his mouth that he wasn't a boy, but, like me, she refused to acknowledge her son and his feelings, and went on a mission to try to change him—a mission that failed miserably.

My tears flowed through the night as I pondered all that I'd heard on that show, but by the next morning, I willed myself to pull it together. Their testimonies were a lightning rod for me—a bolt of common sense and reality that jolted my very foundation. EJ, I concluded, wasn't the problem. The way he was behaving wasn't wrong. Changing his behavior and demanding he act like someone other than whom God created was not sound parenting. In addition to teaching, disciplining, and protecting my son, loving him from the top of his head to the bottom of his little toes, assuring his happiness and shielding him from the righteous indignation and hate of those who refused to accept him was supposed to be my mission. *This is who EJ is,* I declared to myself. *Leave him alone! That's who he wants to be. Why am I trying to change him?*

From that moment forward, I got out of my EJ's way and allowed him what he most craved: his freedom to just . . . be.

· *Loving and Accepting Our Son* ·

When it comes to parenting, Earvin was always the traditional one. That's the way he was raised: his father was in charge and in control, and his kids, Earvin included, knew to respect what he said and do as told. Earvin, in turn, conducted himself in much the same way with our children; he took them to parties, watched over them, and gave them instruction on how to behave and treat others, but he didn't play, either. Earvin was always the disciplinarian of the family; I was the pushover. When the kids were in trouble, they had to answer to him. We had a solid "good cop, bad cop" partnership that way.

Beyond a very quick conversation with him when EJ was little and first started gravitating toward the princess costumes, I never really talked to Earvin about our son's gender preference or feminine proclivities. To be fair, I don't know too many parents who truly consider such things; very few of us want to think about our children's sexuality. We can barely bring ourselves to teach our children to call their private body parts by their real names, let alone consider what they'll be doing with them when they're of age and out on their own and—gasp!—having sex. Our conversations about sexuality are virtually nonexistent until our children become teens, and then the talks tend to begin and end with warnings about sexual disaster: "Have sex and you'll end up a teen parent," and "Have sex and you're going to get a venereal disease," and "If you get drunk at that party, someone might try to rape you." It takes quite some time before we get to the point where we can talk to our kids about having a good, healthy sex life—if we ever get there at all. Earvin and I were no different: our children and sex was not a hot topic in our home to begin with, and we certainly weren't going to powwow over whether our son wanted to be a girl or was gay. I knew, too, that Earvin would not approve of my decision to allow EJ to express himself the way he wanted to and play the way he wanted to play. Earvin was the typical alpha male, and he believed that if we, as parents, were strict enough and guided EJ toward more traditional gender play and roles, he could be changed. Truly, he believed all EJ needed was a little toughening up. Earvin did not see what I saw—that we were looking at the core and spirit of who EJ was.

So I hid it from my husband. I would buy EJ Barbie dolls for Christmas and let him play with them in his room, out of his father's presence. He was especially drawn to the special-edition dolls fashioned after Disney villains, like Cruella De Vil from *101 Dalmations* and Ursula from *The Little Mermaid*. They had capes, dramatic makeup, and attitudes. Swagger. That's exactly what EJ loved, and he would stay in his room for hours, dressing them up, making up stories, characters, and plots, and just enjoying reveling in his own imagination.

When he wasn't playing with the dolls, I kept them in my closet, in the original boxes, not only so that these collector's items would stay reasonably preserved, but because they would help me cover for my son by making Earvin believe they really were for me. If EJ couldn't access the Barbies in my closet, he would simply go into his sister's room—she was old enough by then to have and play with her own baby dolls—and play with hers or join in while she played.

This worked for quite some time, too, until Earvin popped into EJ's room one day and caught him midplay. His ire was swift, direct, and devastating. Earvin snatched the dolls, then called all of us to EJ's room—me, Elisa, the housekeeper, and EJ—for a one-sided family "discussion."

"I want you to take all these dolls out of this room right now," he said, his voice quiet but forceful. He pushed the dolls in my direction; I slowly took them into my hands. "I don't want EJ playing with these dolls anymore. Boys don't do that."

I felt absolutely horrible. EJ, heartbroken, cried and cried, and all I could do was watch it. In that moment, I felt like I had to honor my husband's wishes, despite that doing so hurt my child and, by extension, me. But there was no talking to him reasonably about this thing; Earvin was so upset, particularly with me. "Why are you doing this?" he asked as I packed away the dolls and put them on the shelf at the top of my closet (where they remain to this day). "He's never going to stop if you keep allowing him to do this!"

"Earvin, I tried to stop it," I insisted. "I tried everything—buying him trucks, having him play with other boys, hiding the dolls, telling him that he needed to play like a boy. None of it works because this is what he wants to do. This is what he likes."

Still, Earvin wouldn't hear of it. He didn't want to. And that was the end of the discussion as far as he was concerned. "Don't do it again," he said, seething, before leaving the room abruptly.

But I couldn't stop myself. I am a mother, with a well of emotion running deep in my veins. I couldn't bear to watch my son cry and mope around the house, sad because his father wouldn't allow him the indulgence of being exactly who he was. My mother's heart thought it unfathomable that we, as his parents, would deny our child his joy. For me, EJ's behavior wasn't about presentation of a specific gender or his sexuality or whether or not he was attracted to boys or girls. It was about having the freedom to be with his friends and play video games or dress up dolls or roll a truck across the floor or twirl around in a skirt and be the kind of kid who was genuinely happy. Why wouldn't I want my child to be at his happiest? My job as his mother was to protect him—to keep him safe from ridicule and judgment and encourage him to grow and blossom—not to add to the negativity.

> *My job as his mother was to protect him—to keep him safe from ridicule and judgment and encourage him to grow and blossom—not to add to the negativity.*

So when Earvin wasn't around, I would let EJ play with the Barbies. Later, when he was about nine, I added to his dress-up collection when I introduced him to Build-A-Bear, a store where customers can purchase a stuffed animal, then add clothes and accessories to customize their bears. EJ would always pick a girl bear and dress her up in fancy duds, and I would add boy outfits to the collection so that when he got his bear home around Earvin, he could strip her down and toss on the pants and blue shirts so that "she" looked like a "he." Eventually, EJ had quite the Build-A-Bear collection! And I, in effect, taught my son how to hide. He had specific instructions: "EJ, when you go out in public, you can't be that way, okay?" I'd say. "You can only do this inside our house, when your Dad's away, okay?" It was the only way I could think of that would allow him to be himself and, well, happy. EJ instinctively understood how important it was to work within those parameters and was extremely careful about his natural expression, saving it for home and with his closest friends.

He certainly did have a few friends with whom he could be himself, which I was happy about. We were in an environment, after all, where some of EJ's fellow students had nontraditional homes: one friend had two moms, another friend had two dads, and still another had two moms and was also coparented by her biological father, who, too, was homosexual. One friend in particular, a girl, liked to dress up like a boy and play with boy toys. She and EJ made for an interesting combination: when they had playdates, EJ would bring his boy stuff, she would bring her girly toys, and they would switch and play with each other's things. An added benefit: because she liked sports, video games, and other things typically favored by boys, EJ got quite a bit of "boy play," too.

It was within these parameters and within those types of friendships that EJ found his freedom and I, ultimately, cultivated my understanding and acceptance of my son.

· *No More Hiding* ·

EJ was thirteen when I put him in programs where he didn't have to worry about being judged. One camp in particular, French Woods Festival of the Performing Arts near Hancock, New York, created a welcoming environment where his peers accepted him just as he was and encouraged him to pursue his creative passions. He blossomed there.

Not long after that, we were in Hawaii on a family vacation with a few of our friends when I opened the proverbial closet, took him by his hand, and told him it was okay to come out. That's when I realized, for sure, that our son was gay. We were sitting by the pool when I overheard him and a friend snickering behind a group of boys in bathing suits who'd just passed by. They were catcalling them the same way two mannish heterosexual boys would girls. That's when I knew for sure it was official: my son is gay. He was still changing and growing, but there was no denying it anymore. He wasn't going to snap out of it and be done; this was pretty much who he was. Who he had been all along.

The first chance I got to be alone with EJ, I let the question fly: "Babe, I saw you looking at a guy, and you guys were snickering like you thought he was cute. Does that mean you like boys now?"

EJ got really quiet; he looked frightened. Finally, after a long silence, he said, "I think so."

"You think so or you know so?" I said, being as direct as possible. "It's okay if you are or you're not. I just want you to know that I saw you at the pool, and I'm okay with it."

EJ was quiet again. "I think I do," he said simply.

"Well, then," I said, "it's okay."

"Okay," he said.

"We're all okay?"

"Yeah, Mom, we're okay."

I folded him into a huge embrace and assured him he had my full support, no matter what, and that with me, he could be whoever he wanted to be.

When the kids and I got back home, I told my husband the story. "Maybe I can talk to him," he said, rubbing his brow.

"It is what it is, Earvin," I said. "But I agree we should talk to him."

Earvin insisted on speaking to EJ for himself. "You know, your mother told me that you think you're gay," he said, wasting no time getting to the heart of the matter. "I just want you to know that's not what I thought my son would be and I'm very disappointed. Are you sure this is what you want? Because it's going to be a difficult life, and it's going to be really hard on you.

People will make fun of you. People will be mean to you. Are you sure you're up for that?"

With each word, I could see EJ's shoulders drop a little lower; he hung his head and choked back his words. The sole word he could muster: "Yeah."

"Well," Earvin said, sighing, "I want you to know that I am very disappointed. You are getting ready to go into a lifestyle that's going to be very hard on you, but if this is what you want, go on into it. I love you no matter what, but I don't approve."

Tears welled in EJ's eyes, and I cried, too. I was crushed for him. As Earvin hugged our son, I choked back some choice words of my own; I didn't want to go against my husband in that moment because, no matter how much it hurt, he had the right to express his opinion on the matter. But EJ was barely out the door before I set upon my husband: "I can't believe you just did that!" I yelled.

"He needs to know how hard this life is going to be, Cookie," Earvin insisted. "This is not going to be a piece of cake."

For him and for me, that was that. My husband, the man of few words, had no more to say. I knew enough to know that arguing with him wouldn't change his mind.

The next day, though, I think Earvin's fatherly instincts kicked back in and he realized just how harsh he'd been with our son. Unbeknownst to me, he called EJ into our room and apologized for his initial reaction. I wasn't present when they had the conversation, but Earvin recounted it proudly shortly after he talked with

EJ: "I told him, 'I thought about this and I want you to know that I do love you and I'm very proud of you and I'm sorry for the things I said to you because I don't believe any of that. I want you to be who you're going to be and you have my full support, no matter what. I love you more than anything and I'm very proud of you.'

"Both of us were standing there crying, and I hugged him and let him go," Earvin added.

"Oh my God," I said, crying, too. "I'm so proud of you."

It was such a special moment. Finally, EJ had the full support of *both* his parents to be himself.

I'm sure there are a lot of things EJ's never told me about his experiences, and frankly, I don't want to know the details. But I've always wanted the kind of relationship with my children that made clear to them that if there's something big in their lives, we can talk about it. They honor me with that blessing. In this case, when it came to EJ's sexuality, I wanted to break the ice first because I wanted him—needed him—to understand that he can still be in this family while being exactly who he is. I'm not going to lie: a part of that thinking did come from a bit of mom guilt after teaching him how to hide his true self from others. But I didn't want him to walk into adulthood that way—hiding. I was called to release him of that burden.

But, according to my church, it was an abomination and God didn't approve of it. I'd heard countless sermons in which preachers taught about God's destruction of Sodom and Gomorrah because of gay sex and how man is never to lay with man, and I believed it true because I'm a believer and I read it in the Bible for myself.

But as I watched EJ's behavior, I had a hard time embracing those teachings, and I went back and forth with it many times. Indeed, this was the hardest struggle with me because all that I'd been taught was that God would not approve and I shouldn't, either. Still, I'm EJ's mother, and I know for sure that his sexuality was not a choice for him: it is part of his DNA. This is who he has always been. You cannot rinse out his blood to change him. You cannot give him a pill to fix him. You cannot beat it out of him. You are who you are and that is, simply, who you are. I would rather he be exactly who he is rather than to fake it for the sake of others, or live a life so miserable, he takes his own to escape the pain that comes with hiding his true self. We've seen this happen before.

Love is the greatest gift God's given us and, as a mother, it is the greatest gift I could give to my children.

So how did I reconcile my religious beliefs with my son's homosexuality? I struggled; I believe in God's word, but I also believe that sometimes, you have to take it right to Him. I prayed about it, and what God put in my heart was this: "Love your child." That's what I heard. Love is the greatest gift God's given us and, as a mother, it is the greatest gift I could give to my children. And so that is what I do. That is what Earvin and I do.

Love was at the very center of how we chose to deal with the press a few years back when TMZ tried to out EJ to the world. The website posted a video of our son holding hands with his best friend, Alessandro, and proclaimed he was stepping out for the first time with his "boyfriend." Soon enough, media outlets were feeding on the story and rushing to confirm that EJ was, indeed, homosexual. It was a little scary for about a half second, because the press tried to make a big deal out of it. Frankly, we were worried that someone would try to hurt our son, and EJ feared that the story might affect his father's image, which was the last thing he wanted to do. Earvin decided to get ahead of the press by making a statement and being done with it. "Listen, I'm just going to go out there and tell them I support EJ and that's that," Earvin said. "Whatever happens after that, we don't care."

I could see the relief wash over EJ's body; he knew his father had his back. Earvin was widely praised for his sweet, loving words: "I love EJ so much, that's my main man," he said. "I think he really wanted to be out. But he was torn. He just didn't know how. He just said, 'This is my moment. This is my time. I'm happy to share with the world who I am.' And I said, 'Go, EJ, go.'"

He added: "I'm behind him a million percent. This is really wonderful for him."

It most certainly is.

Chapter Nine

All in the Family: Adopting Elisa

W hen Earvin and I imagined our life together and painted pictures in our minds of what it would look like, there were always babies. Always. Our reasons were as typical and pure as those of most couples who choose to be parents: we wanted a family because we were in love and wanted to have a living testament to our devotion to each other and to God. We'd always envisioned a house full of joy and laughter with little ones who would help us create memories that would last a lifetime. We wanted to carry on the legacy of the Johnson name, and we wanted to grow old together, surrounded by family. We were blessed to find each of these things with EJ, and, of course, we built this, too, with Andre, Earvin's son from a prior relationship, but we didn't want to stop there. We wanted to expand our family.

Doing this naturally, though, was not an option for us, not with the deadly virus coursing through Earvin's blood. Today, medical advances have made it so that couples can become parents without passing along the virus to their partners and their babies; prospective fathers infected with HIV can have their sperm washed free of the virus before it's inserted into a woman, and HIV-infected women can take antiretroviral drugs during their pregnancy and at labor and delivery to avoid infecting their babies. But these are developments that no one dreamed possible when we were planning our family. Back then, in the early 1990s, researchers were still trying to figure out how to keep HIV-infected humans from getting full-blown AIDS; hardly anyone could imagine a day when someone with the virus could procreate without passing it along to a partner and their baby, much less conjure up ways to help couples do so successfully. Everyone, including those in the medical establishment, still thought HIV was a death sentence and that anyone who had unprotected sex with an infected partner was, in essence, committing suicide.

We wanted a family because we were in love and wanted to have a living testament to our devotion to each other and to God.

Earvin and I had so much to live for, and we wanted to share our world with an extended family of our own. Of course, it hurt my heart to know that I would never feel another baby in my belly. I wanted to make more babies with my husband, but at that moment, it wasn't an option for us. So while we held out hope that medicine eventually would allow us to make a baby the traditional way, we grew our family the only way possible for us at that time: we agreed to adopt.

This had long been more than a notion for us. Earlier in our relationship, when we were talking about the life we would build together, we'd always agreed that we would adopt a child. We even thought we might adopt twins. It was just something we wanted to do, and when we were ready to have another child, we decided to adopt.

Being in the public eye called for a level of privacy and protection we could only get by hiring an adoption attorney who could act as our proxy to make sure that we not only became the proud parents of a beautiful baby girl, but also that she came from parents willing to submit to a closed adoption and who would not try to take advantage of us. We were, after all, a high-profile couple who wanted to open our hearts, arms, and home to a child, and key details on our application made it pretty clear who we were, making a closed adoption tough. Though we did not have to reveal our names, Earvin did have to list his profession as athlete and, by law, he had to inform prospective birth parents that he was HIV-positive. Those two details practically screamed, "Earvin and Cookie Johnson want your baby." Frankly, that scared me. I was concerned that one day my baby's birth parents would show up and try to claim my child, ripping our bond to shreds. I was frightened, too, that our celebrity and financial status would make us vulnerable to the monetary whims of birth parents who might have thought that giving their baby to us would give them license to dig into our pockets. Discretion was key for our emotional, mental, physical, and financial safety.

Our private attorney delivered in spades. He put out a query on our behalf in October and within a month, he had found our baby. "She's not sure when she's due," he said. "She's a young girl right out of high school trying to go to college. She's a singer. She lives in Baltimore but can't afford to raise a baby and she's willing to give birth here in Los Angeles, where she has family. What do you think?"

She was, in our estimation, perfect.

And not more than a few weeks later, while we were in the middle of a massive house renovation, with two-year-old EJ settling into toddlerhood, and Christmas just days away, we got the call: our daughter's birth mom was in labor. I'll be honest: I wasn't ready. We knew she was in the last trimester of her pregnancy, but we simply weren't expecting that she was that close to delivery. I had nothing, really: I still had EJ's crib and my best friend, Sharon, let me borrow her bassinet, but beyond that, we did not have much else—no bottles, no clothes, no car seat, no toys, nothing. At first, I was elated, and then a sort of panic set in. My emotions were all over the place; I was buying all manner of baby things and stressing about whether the birth mother would follow through on her promise to let us adopt our daughter. I had good reason to worry: because she had a C-section, we had to wait three long days before we could take full custody of the baby. By law, the baby's mother was not allowed to hand her over until she was able to physically get up from her bed and go to an office to sign the adoption papers—actions that weren't possible until she healed from surgery. So for three days, I paced and shopped and worried and paced some more. Finally, Earvin had had enough: "Cookie, everything is going to be okay. The baby will be here. Stop worrying," he said in his ever-present no-fuss ease. Never one to get riled, Earvin was always the calming presence to my frenetic nervousness. In that moment, his soothing, reassuring voice made me know everything was going to work out just fine.

I tried, and mostly I hid my fear from Earvin and heaped my nervousness on my mother, sister, and best friend, who indulged my anxiety. Sharon, bless her heart, acted as my personal surrogate, sneaking into the hospital nursery to check out the little girl who, because of the closed adoption, I couldn't go visit. For two days, Sharon went up to that hospital, peeked into her little crib, and then called me from her phone with the blow-by-blow: "She's so beautiful, Cookie!" she exclaimed. "She has a red skin tone and a ton of dark, straight black hair and chubby cheeks. She's lovely."

I was going to send Sharon back a third day, but before my friend could get to the hospital, the call came in: our baby's birth mother signed the adoption papers, and we were free to bring her home. Words simply cannot describe the joy we felt knowing that our daughter was on her way to us—on her way to our arms. My heart was ready to burst. To help us avoid a public spectacle, the social worker graciously agreed to bring our baby to our home; it seemed like Earvin, EJ, my mom, and I waited in our kitchen for hours, listening for the doorbell.

Then, finally, she was home.

Earvin answered the door, collected our daughter in her carrier from the social worker, and brought her into the kitchen, where my mom and EJ stood with me, anxious to meet our baby for the first time. And when Earvin rounded that corner and set our baby's carrier on the counter and I peeked under the massive mound of blankets and saw that sweet, sugarpie face, I fell hopelessly, helplessly, totally in love.

> *Words simply cannot describe the joy we felt knowing that our daughter was on her way to us— on her way to our arms. My heart was ready to burst.*

The oohs and ahhs and coos were endless as Earvin and I wiggled our baby, whom we named Elise so that her initials, EJ, could match those of everyone else's in her new immediate family. EJ stood wide-eyed at my side, excited to meet his new little sister. "Look at the new baby," I said, bending down so that he could see our soft bundle of goodness up close. "Her name is Elise."

"Ohmigosh, she's so cute!" he squealed with his baby words and wide smile matching every other giggle in the room. For some reason, he kept calling the baby Elisa, and no matter how much we tried to correct him, he said it again and again. Finally, Earvin and I just went with it, taking away the *e* and adding the *a* to the end of our new baby's name. EJ is the reason his sister's name is Elisa.

I laughed. "This is your new sister," I said, snuggling her neck, touching her fingers, and rocking her in my arms. Truly, it was a perfect moment.

After a few more minutes of unfettered elation and attention heaped on the baby, EJ had had his fill. "Okay, Mommy, you can give her back now," he said, his little brows furrowed. He was done with it all. "Put her back in the thing and give her back to the lady now."

The room erupted into laughter. This was to be expected. EJ, after all, had had his parents to himself for two and a half years, and the entrance of a new sibling—competition—after a very simple ring of the doorbell was hard for my firstborn to grasp. We'd talked to him about it, of course, but there was nothing like seeing it all play out in real time, right before his eyes.

"No, honey," I said, trying to hold back my laughter. "This is your new sister. This is your baby. We can't give her back anymore."

He stared a little harder but said no more. And after a few minutes, EJ was okay. He was never mean to her, never threw a tantrum, never again asked for her to be given back. From that moment forward, he accepted her as his little sister.

And from that moment forward, we thought of her as nothing less than our daughter. She was ours. We were hers. We were a family. And that's all there was to that.

· *Do You Know My Mother?* ·

Elisa was five years old when she started asking me what it was like for me to carry her in my tummy. The question was perfectly natural; she was in kindergarten, and a few of her classmates had moms who were pregnant. It wasn't long before she was asking why those mommies had such fat bellies, and how little babies got inside them and, of course, how I felt carrying her in my own stomach. Simply put: I didn't want to lie to our daughter. First, that's not who I am. I always want my children to count on me for the truth. Plus, we went into the adoption process knowing that we'd have to tell her one day; because we were high-profile people, the chances of keeping Elisa's adoption a secret from her was virtually impossible. The entire world knew I wasn't pregnant with her, after all, and it was only a matter of time before someone—a classmate, a relative, a gossip columnist, a TV show—would reveal the details of how she became a part of our family. So we planned to tell our daughter she was adopted with the hope that she'd be protected from the shock of being told by someone other than us.

I read up on how to break the news, and every source I consulted suggested I keep the conversation and details short and sweet: I was to tell her as much as she needed to know, when she wanted to know it. That moment came one day while she was in her room, playing with her dolls. "Mommy," she asked innocently, "what was I like when I was in your tummy?"

I took a deep breath, braced myself, and tried to be matter-of-fact in my answer, with the hope that responding easily would keep her from getting upset by the news. "You were never in my tummy," I told her. "Most mommies don't know what their babes are going to look like, but we were very lucky because we got to choose you. We wanted a pretty little girl, and we fell in love with you right away because we chose you."

She was quiet for a moment. "You chose me?" she asked as she ran a brush through her doll's head.

"Yes, we chose you," I said. "And we're a happy family."

Seemingly content with the answer, Elisa went back to brushing her doll's hair, and we didn't talk about it further. But a few months later, she brought up the subject again, this time with her father. "Daddy, did you know I was adopted?" she asked.

Earvin laughed a little, and then scooped her up into his arms. "Of course, I know that, baby," he said. "But you'll always be my little girl. Daddy loves you so much."

And we didn't talk about it anymore. That was enough for five-year-old Elisa.

But eight-year-old Elisa was much more curious, a lot more observant, and way more demanding than kindergarten Elisa; this time, when she started seeing the pregnant mothers of her classmates waddling through the school hallway, she wanted to know a bit more about where she came from. Ditto when we'd be out shopping or traveling and people who didn't know we adopted would take stock of who in our family looked like whom: "Wow," they'd say, "Elisa looks just like Magic, and EJ looks exactly like you!" She and I would just snicker and say, "Thank you!" That was our little joke.

But as our daughter made the long stretch to puberty, she began to want more solid information about her birth family. She wanted to know who she looked like, how we came to "choose" her, and details on the young woman whose belly she filled: where her personality came from, whose toes resembled her own, and whether she had siblings, cousins, and grandparents who knew about her and missed her, too. Elisa wanted to know why her mother gave her away. Finally, she drilled me for the information she craved.

"Mom," she asked, "have you ever seen a picture of my mother?"

My heart raced. "Yes," I answered slowly. "I have."

"What does she look like?" Elisa asked, leaning in, wide-eyed.

"Well, from what I remember from the photo, she looks a lot like you," I said.

Elisa stared some more and continued: "What else do you know about her? I mean, what was she like?"

"I don't know a whole lot, Elisa. But I do know she has an identical twin sister," I said.

"Do you know anything about my father?"

Because it was her birth mother who filled out the paperwork at the adoption agency, I knew far less about the father, but I told Elisa the basics of what I knew. "I believe he was an athlete in high school," I said.

That small amount of information couldn't satisfy our daughter; it only led to more questions, even for her brothers. EJ told me that she'd asked him repeatedly, "Do you think I'll ever get to meet them?"

I admit I didn't have the tools to ease Elisa's suffering. Earvin and I gave birth to our unconditional love for her, and Elisa loved us all the same, but the pull to know her birth mom and the circumstances behind her adoption bordered on obsessive. Granted, that's the kind of personality Elisa has; once she gets a bug in her brain about any one particular thing, she will fixate on it until she is wholly satisfied. This goes for friends. Suitors. Exes. Any and all decisions she makes during the course of the day. All of it. But in the case of her birth family, truly, she'd become consumed with the impulse to know the full story.

Recognizing her craving, I decided it was time to reveal to her what I'd locked away in my safe since before she was born: the one photo of her parents that we'd received during the closed adoption process.

"I'm going to show her the picture," I told Earvin one morning, not long before Elisa's thirteenth birthday. "She keeps asking about them."

"You sure you want to do that?" he asked. "I just wonder if it's going to open a can of worms."

"Well," I said, "I'll just show her the picture and that'll be it. I won't give her their names."

I tucked that picture in a beautiful gold frame, put the frame into a box that I wrapped with birthday paper and a giant bow, and I put it away for just the right moment. It came the day after we celebrated Elisa's thirteenth birthday with a dance party at our house, when the excitement of becoming a teenager climaxed and the people who loved Elisa with abandon—me, EJ, my sister, Pat—were chilling out, enjoying one another's company. "Elisa, I have something for you," I said, standing up. "I'll be right back."

I ran upstairs and pulled the box from the corner of my bedroom closet where I'd tucked it away. I was so excited about the moment, and I just knew she would be, too, once she opened this special present. "This is for you," I said, handing the box to her.

Elisa stared at the box, then at me, then back at the box. "What is it, Mom?" she asked.

"Well, open it and see," I said simply, smiling.

Elisa carefully removed the lid and lifted out the frame. She gazed at the photograph, and then let out a gasp. "Oh my God," she said, her voice trembling. "Is this *them?*"

I nodded.

The photo, tattered around the edges, was an old prom picture of Elisa's birth parents. In it, the birth mother wore a long black dress; her father, by her side, rocked a black tux. Both were smiling broadly, flashing the same bright, perfect teeth Elisa has. Their faces offered the physical evidence of Elisa's origins: she had her dad's coloring and skin tone, but all of her other features—her nose, her eyes, her petite figure—are nearly identical to her birth mom's. The way the couple was posed, standing closely together, made the mom's baby bump less visible, but discerning eyes could catch it: that was Elisa

Right there, in that picture, was the first tangible connection Elisa had to the people who gave her life.

in her stomach. Right there, in that picture, was the first tangible connection Elisa had to the people who gave her life.

The room fell silent as Elisa studied the photo, peering into the face of the woman who so closely resembled her that it must have been like looking in the mirror. And then, suddenly, Elisa burst into tears and bolted upstairs to her room.

One thought ran through my head: *Oh my Lord, what was I thinking?*

I waited a beat before I made my way up the stairs to talk to her, knowing that what I said would be critical not only to calming my daughter but also to helping her—and me—move forward. I cracked open her bedroom door and poked my head in. "Elisa?"

She was lying across the bed, sobbing into a pillow. The picture lay next to her.

"I'm so sorry," I said as I sat on the edge of the bed and began softly rubbing her back. "I didn't want to hurt you. Why are you crying?"

"I just never thought I'd see them!" she said, wailing. "I can't believe how much I look like her. And that means I really don't look like you!"

It's one thing to know you're adopted; it's a totally different thing to actually see the faces of the two people who created and birthed you. Questions about identity, particularly at an age when early teenagers are already struggling to figure out who exactly they are, can only be compounded when an adopted child also must consider the DNA that flows through her veins and to where, exactly, her ancestral lines morph and stretch. Finally, Elisa was seeing evidence of her origins—evidence that there were, indeed, two people on the planet who carried her blood.

She was overwhelmed.

I was scared.

I gently pulled Elisa up toward me and hugged her tightly. "I want you to know something," I whispered. "You will always be mine. She's the woman who gave you birth. That's it. But you are a part of this family. You laugh like us. You talk like us. You think like us. You *are* us."

"I know that, Mommy," she said. "But do you know where they are?"

I didn't answer right away. I had an idea of where her parents were, but I wasn't ready for her to know that yet. The idea of her searching for her birth parents overwhelmed me, not only because I was afraid she'd reject our family for her blood relatives, but also because I didn't think my daughter could handle the emotional juggle required to seek out her birth family and deal with the consequences of rejection by the parents who put her up for adoption. Still, she craved that information. I gave her details I thought were safe enough for her to manage.

"I don't have a lot more information," I said. "But I can tell you their first names." I did, and that brought on a whole new round of tears.

"Will I ever get to meet them?" she asked, finally.

"I'm not opposed to you meeting them," I told my daughter, "but it's not the right time yet. We'll do that when you're eighteen."

Elisa bolted upright and looked directly at me. "We will?" she asked.

"Yes, we will," I repeated.

The following day, Earvin chimed in with his own reassurances and reminders for Elisa. He pulled her onto his lap and looked her in her sweet little face. "One day, you'll get to meet your birth parents and know them," he told her, his voice tender. "We've always wanted that for you. But as your father, I want you to understand something: no man on this earth is ever going to love you as much as I do." And with that, he gave our daughter a big kiss.

"Thanks, Daddy," Elisa said as she fell into her father's embrace.

Elisa kept that framed photo on her nightstand and relished showing it off to friends who came to our house to visit. "Wow," they'd say, "it's crazy how much you look like her!"

"Right?" she'd say. "I can't believe it, either."

Her preoccupation with the photo lasted several weeks, but once the initial shock of seeing their faces finally wore off, things got back to normal.

Normal, that is, until Elisa turned sixteen. That's when everything spiraled out of control.

· The True Meaning of Motherhood ·

It started when Elisa's birth mom had a friend reach out to his distant cousin—our longtime personal driver, Donald. The man sent a Facebook message to Donald stating the case for why we should upend our closed adoption agreement, meet with the birth mom, and, ultimately, support reuniting her with the daughter she'd given to us sixteen years prior. Every concern I had about revealing in the adoption papers Earvin's HIV status and job as a professional basketball player had finally caught up with us: the birth parents knew all along that we'd adopted their baby, and now the birth mother wanted to toss out her promise not to contact us and our child.

The timing was no coincidence; just a week before Donald got that message, Earvin and I had thrown Elisa a Sweet Sixteen birthday celebration at the House of Blues in Los Angeles—a party that rivaled the soirees highlighted on the then-popular, now-defunct MTV show *My Super Sweet 16*. It was an incredibly elaborate affair attended by dozens of Elisa's friends, with a huge surprise organized by her dad: musical performances by Snoop Dogg, Chris Brown, and Tiga. When Snoop walked onto that stage, Elisa was absolutely beside herself, and she left a footprint of her excitement all across social media, on her Facebook, Twitter, and Instagram pages, for the world to see. Her birth mom caught a glimpse and made her move.

Donald told Earvin about her volley first. "I got a message from Elisa's birth mother," he said. "Apparently, she really wants to get in touch with Elisa."

"What do you mean?" Earvin asked.

Donald explained the familial connection and the Facebook message he'd received. "My cousin says the mother has been talking about how much she wants to reunite with Elisa. She saw photos of her from the party."

Earvin peered at him for a long moment and then finally stated definitively, "That's not something I can give you an answer about right now. Cookie and I need to discuss that."

We did. Earvin had barely pushed the words through his lips before I said, "Absolutely not." Understand, it's not that I wanted to keep secrets from our daughter or deny the natural connection between her and her birth mom; it's just that I didn't think my daughter, a natural empathizer who carried her emotions like a weight around her neck, could handle an introduction at that specific moment. She was in the eleventh grade, an incredibly important year in which she had to make sure her grades, SAT scores, and extracurricular activities were on point for her college applications. The last thing I wanted to heap onto her responsibilities was the drama that would surely come if she were to dive into a relationship with her birth family.

Truthfully, I wasn't ready for it, either. I wasn't convinced that the birth mom, inspired by the lavish party we threw for Elisa, wasn't looking for a financial come-up. What's more, I wasn't ready to handle the emotional toll that would come with managing my daughter's feelings and some of my own. After all, she was asking for me to hand over my daughter, my heart, my love; I was afraid our daughter would fall madly in love with her birth family and abandon us—that she would devote every spare moment to getting to know them and forget that we'd loved her, raised her, disciplined her, and wanted her.

Sure, this is hard to admit, but I don't doubt for a second that my reaction was human.

"You know what you can have Donald tell her?" I said to Earvin. "We can do an introduction, but she'll have to wait until Elisa is eighteen. That's what I promised our daughter, and we're going to stick to that."

And that was that, as far as I was concerned. Still, our daughter's birth mom persisted, personally connecting with Donald on Facebook, sharing family pictures and YouTube videos of songs she'd written and sung for Elisa, and even connecting Donald with Elisa's grandfather in Los Angeles. Earvin had asked Donald to cease communication with her, but Donald continued anyway, a defiance that would have gotten him fired had he not been with us for so long and, as far as we were concerned, a part of our family. Still, I was bothered that she was so close and working so hard to get into Elisa's life.

A few times after that, Elisa did ask me about meeting her birth mother, and every time she did, I'd reassure her that we would pursue it when she turned eighteen. "We just want you to stay focused on your studies right now," I told her. "You've got to keep up your grades, focus on your SATs, and get ready for college. This is such a critical year for you—and I don't want you to get distracted."

Still, she persisted. I found out many years later that her obsession was fueled by her big brother, Andre, who, after coming to live with us for a while during his teens, had told Elisa that her birth mom had reached out. She never connected with her, though, as far as I know, until when I said it would be best. Within days of her eighteenth birthday on December 21, 2012, Elisa made her desire to meet her mom known. "Can we do it soon, Mom?" she pressed.

"Yes," I assured her. "But I want to get through your prom and graduation first. Once everything settles down, we can look into it."

In the meantime, Earvin and I decided to call the birth mom to feel her out and make sure that it was safe to introduce our daughter to her. Donald got her number to us, and we quickly reached out. I talked to her first. "So," I said, searching for the right way to start such an awkward conversation, "we know you've been wanting to meet Elisa."

"Yes, that's something I'd really love to do," she quickly offered.

"Okay, well, we just wanted to talk to you first," I told her. "Can you tell us a little bit about what's been happening in your life and why you want to meet her at this point?"

She was a barrel of waterworks—just like Elisa. "Well," she said, her voice cracking, "I understand that this was supposed to be a closed adoption. I've just reached a point in my life where I really feel like I have to meet Elisa. I've even talked to my pastor about it. He encouraged me to reach out."

From there, she gushed what seemed like her entire life story: she and Elisa's birth father were high school sweethearts—he, a star football player, she a cheerleader. When she got pregnant, neither they nor their families could afford to provide for their child, so she made the most difficult choice of her life: she put Elisa up for adoption. "Back in those days, Elisa's dad and I were crazy about each other," she said, adding that the two also had a teenage son together. "But as much as I wanted the relationship, things between us just didn't work out."

Long after their romance ended, the mother fell in love with and married a man she met in church; together, they had a baby girl who, at the time of our call, was just a few months old. "All these years," she said, still crying, "I've never stopped thinking about Elisa. Ever since I gave her up, I felt like a part of me was missing, and I've never been able to fill that void."

Listening to her speak was like listening to my daughter: she and Elisa had the same personality, the same level of emotion, the same energy. And, like Elisa, she couldn't move forward without dealing with the emptiness that came with the adoption separation. My motherly instincts were really clear about this one true thing: this woman was warm, genuine. Trustworthy. That she was in the church was a huge bonus. By the end of my time with her on that call, I knew that arranging a reunion between her and Elisa would be safe for my daughter and, ultimately, our family. Earvin agreed and wrapped up the call by giving her our blessing.

"It was always our plan for Elisa to meet you one day," he said simply. "We never wanted to hold that back from her. But there's just one last thing I want to say before we let you go." Earvin took a beat and leaned in a little closer to the phone. "Please don't hurt my baby," he said softly. His voice was even, but firm; his tone relayed that he meant business. "We love her so much."

She said she understood. "I will not hurt her," she added, her voice cracking. "I'm not asking anything from Elisa. I just want to see her again."

The next day, we told Elisa about the call and, in typical Elisa fashion, there were major waterworks—enough to make me feel like maybe she wasn't ready. "Elisa, are you sure you're ready for this?" I asked her.

"I am," she said, sniffling, "but I'm also scared. I have mixed feelings."

Her fear was far outweighed by her curiosity. Through her tears, and armed for the first time ever with the names of both her parents, she went straight to her computer and consulted Google for all the information she could scrounge up on them. The first thing she found was a YouTube video of the sad song her birth mom made about loss and longing.

You guessed it: Elisa burst into tears. "I know that song is to me," she said, sniffling.

I fed Elisa more clues: "She also told me that she has a son and a baby girl," I said, rubbing Elisa's back.

Through more tears, she scrolled through images she found on her birth mother's Facebook page. She gasped loudly when she clicked through a series of pictures of a young man, a few years her junior. "Oh my God!" she exclaimed.

"What?" I asked, leaning into the computer.

"Mom, that boy is my full brother!"

"No, it isn't," I said, squinting at the picture.

"Yes! Yes, it is!" she said. "Look at him. I see her in his face, and I see my birth father in it, too. Look at him," she demanded. "Now look at me."

Finally, my daughter had at her fingertips what she'd longed for since the moment I told her that she was adopted: connection to her beginning.

Later, she discovered the name of her birth mom's twin. "I know that name from somewhere!" she exclaimed. After thinking about it for a few minutes, it hit her: the sister had been following her on social media and had even posted a few comments on Elisa's Instagram page, including, "Congratulations, we're so happy for you," on a photo of my daughter's Sweet Sixteen party. Elisa said she'd wondered who'd posted the comment, never once imagining it could be a relative. The thought left her uneasy. "Have they been stalking me or something?" Elisa asked. "This is getting creepy. I don't know if I want to meet them anymore."

That wasn't really an option; we'd come too far to turn back now. "We're going to do this," I said, assuring her.

I did think it important, though, to get Elisa some advice on how to handle this monumental step in her adoption journey. Frankly, I needed some for myself, too. So many fears pierced my thoughts: what if my daughter liked her birth mother better than she did me? What if they bonded? Would I lose her?

"Be prepared," said the therapist, who, himself a child of adoption, was adept at explaining all the different emotions that would bubble up as our family connected with Elisa's birth family. I needed to prepare, he said, for Elisa wanting to spend a lot of time with them—a natural reaction to finally being able to bond with someone she'd been curious about for so long. "You just have to be patient with her and relax."

What if my daughter liked her birth mother better than she did me? What if they bonded? Would I lose her?

Relax. I didn't think that was at all possible in such an intense situation, which could have torn apart the bond I had with my daughter.

I never relayed my fear to Elisa, but she sensed it. "Mommy, don't worry," she'd say, reassuring me. "Nothing will change between us. You'll always be my best friend."

When we finally felt the time was right for an in-person meeting, Elisa's therapist recommended we travel to the birth mom's home city so that if things didn't go well, Elisa wouldn't be left with a bad feeling about her own home city. Earvin decided not to go to the meeting; he felt strongly that if he were present, he'd influence our daughter's opinion of her birth mom. "As her father, I'm so competitive and protective that if I go, it'll change everything," he told me. "If anything is said that might hurt her, I know myself: I will jump in," he said.

So Elisa and I headed for Baltimore, with my sister, Pat, riding shotgun for support. The plan was for the birth mother, her husband, and their new baby to meet us in our hotel room.

But all those therapy sessions and thoughtful planning did nothing to ease our anxiety; both Elisa and I were nervous wrecks. She fretted about what she should wear; I was consumed with how it would feel to see the woman for the first time. After Elisa finally settled on an outfit—she chose jeans and a comfortable sweatshirt—she sat on the couch in our room's living area. I saddled up next to her. "We'll get through this," I told her. Really, I was talking to myself as much as I was to her.

Moments later, the phone rang: they were in the hotel lobby. Pat, no doubt sensing how on edge I was, agreed to go meet them and bring them back to our room, so that Elisa and I could have a few more minutes preparing ourselves. But one could never really be prepared for such a meeting; when she heard Pat's key in the door, Elisa gripped the arm of the couch so hard, her knuckles looked like they'd pop out of her skin. I rubbed her thigh, hoping not only to settle her, but myself, too. Pat opened the door, the couple stepped inside, and for a split second, time stood still. None of us moved. We all just stared.

The birth mom looked even more like Elisa in person than she had in the prom photo. She sported a short Afro, and was as thin as my daughter, maybe even tinier. It was hard to believe she'd just had a baby, much less was the mom of three.

"Hello," she said, nervously. She looked over in Elisa's direction and smiled. "This is my husband."

"Oh, hi," Elisa mumbled. She scooted even closer to me.

The mother, probably not wanting to impose or make the moment even more awkward, didn't try to hug Elisa. Instead, she sat down on the couch across from us, with the baby on her lap. Thank God, her baby girl was with her; it gave us a way to break the ice.

"She's so cute!" I blurted out.

"Thank you!" she said.

Elisa was now so close to my body she was practically glued to my side; she'd hardly said a word. The husband kept the conversation going with small talk, but finally, when the mother settled in, she started sharing the missing pieces Elisa had long longed for. Her mother, she explained, had issues at the time and couldn't care for her twin sister and her, so she left them to be raised by their paternal grandmother. She got pregnant with Elisa in high school and wanted to keep her baby, but her grandmother said she simply couldn't raise any more kids. She had one of two choices: keep the baby and move hundreds of miles away to California with her father, a struggling musician who traveled a lot and would not be able to help with the baby, or give up her baby for adoption. "I really never wanted to give you up, Elisa," she said, a tear sliding down her cheek. She wiped it with the back of her hand and continued, her voice cracking. "When I put you up for adoption, I just felt like it was the only real choice I had."

Her words hung in the air, thick and dark. Finally, Elisa spoke; she was all business. "After the two of you separated," she asked, "did my birth father have any other children, and is he married now?"

The birth mom hesitated. "Well," she finally said, "hold on—now let me count. Which one of his kids do you want to know about?"

We all cracked up; her joke immediately cut the tension.

"No, but seriously, your father isn't married. But he did have many other children."

"Your son, do he and I have the same father?" Elisa asked. Her birth mom nodded. Elisa's eyes widened. "How old is my brother, the son you guys had?"

"He's thirteen now," she said. "He's an athlete, just like his father."

Over the next hour, no topic was off-limits. We listened in as the birth mother told us of her life as a child and her accomplishments, including that she loved to sing—a detail that hit home for

Elisa, who also enjoys singing and dreams of becoming a musician. She also revealed that she knew from the beginning that Earvin and I had adopted her baby; the details in the adoption papers were a dead giveaway. "I wanted to reach out to you years ago," she told Elisa, "but I knew we'd agreed to a closed adoption. And I respected that. I tried to move on with my life, but I just got to a point where I couldn't seem to do that. I felt like I needed to see you in order to get some closure."

Elisa hung on her every word, but, surprisingly, she didn't cry.

"Is there anything else you want to know?" she asked.

"Yes," Elisa said. "When can I meet the rest of the family?"

The mother glanced over at me and then back at Elisa. "We can do that soon, even tomorrow. But only if your mother is okay with that."

I was. After all, our initial meeting put me in total ease with the connection she had with my daughter. Even Elisa had loosened up. She recognized what I did, too: these were good people.

"Tomorrow sounds good," I said.

We agreed that she would pick up Elisa around 10:00 a.m., and then we all stood. And finally, Elisa and her birth mother gave each other the biggest hug. "I'm so glad I finally got to see you," she said, tears flooding her face. "Thank you. Thank you so much."

At last, Elisa cried, too.

The next day while she visited with her birth mother's family, Elisa texted me the play-by-play throughout her stay. The twin sister practically tackled her the moment she got out of the car. "She was just crying and crying, Mom!" Elisa texted. A couple hours later: "The grandmother is totally hilarious!" Elisa wrote of her birth mother's mom. Later that afternoon, Elisa also got to spend time with her little brother. "It's weird, but it feels like we've always known each other," she wrote. They clicked instantly over everything from music (they're both into hip-hop) to sports (they both played basketball). That evening, when my daughter came back to the hotel, she was exhausted but relieved and happy.

That was just the beginning of Elisa's connection with the family. Though she left for college a month after the initial meeting, she kept in touch with her birth mom by phone and text and even traveled to her home to attend the baby's first birthday party. It was on that trip that she met her birth father, who stopped by for a brief visit. "He didn't mean to be awkward, but I could tell he was very uncomfortable," Elisa later told me. "He just kind of stood there and looked at me."

Elisa never met any of his other children, and she and her birth father have yet to strike up a relationship.

Elisa is now more confident than I've ever seen her. It's not like she'd be falling apart if she hadn't yet met her birth parents. But now that she knows who they are, she finally has a major piece to her story, which she'd been missing for nearly two decades. Instead of constantly wondering where she came from, she can look ahead. She needed the whole truth in order to move forward. I think we all needed that.

As for my nervousness that I might lose Elisa, the opposite happened: the experience drew us closer together. She does have a good relationship with her birth mom, and I've encouraged her to maintain it; yet their connection is completely separate and different from the one she and I will always share. A conversation we had during one of Elisa's visits to see her birth mom was proof of that.

"Mom," she whispered into her cell phone.

"What is it, honey—and why are you whispering?"

"I'm in the bathroom," she said. "I snuck away in here to call you."

"Is everything okay?" I asked.

"Yes—but she wants me to call her Mom."

I paused. "So what did you tell her?"

"I told her I couldn't do that."

"You did?"

"Yes." And then Elisa uttered a sentence that laid all my fears to rest. "I told her I already have a mom: that's you."

· Chapter Ten ·

The Truth about
Basketball Wives

Tune into "reality" TV, read a blog, watch a gossip show, scroll
through Twitter feeds, listen to the conversation of the average
human who pays any kind of attention at all to pop culture, and
you'd be inclined to think that women married to professional
athletes—NBA players in particular—spend the majority of our
days spilling out of tight dresses while cursing in fancy restaurants,
tossing champagne in one another's faces, tugging at one another's
weaves, and mastering in maximum drama. These days, basketball
wives are more known for being the glamorous mistresses of public mischief than we are for what we truly bring to our high-profile
marriages when the camera isn't watching. Of course, there are
some wild and crazy significant others who get super jealous and
behave badly; this is true of most humans, whether they live in the

spotlight and have huge bank accounts or they're living on the margins with modest means. Still, I can say that what is portrayed on television looks nothing like what I've experienced in my real life being married to one of the game's most high-profile players.

These days, basketball wives are more known for being the glamorous mistresses of public mischief than we are for what we truly bring to our high-profile marriages when the camera isn't watching.

Here's how it worked when I was in the life: the Laker wives had one another's backs and moved as a unit, working together to help keep our families intact as our husbands kept up their rigorous NBA schedules. We threw birthday, anniversary, and graduation parties together, celebrated wins together, ate dinner with one another, and put together playdates for our kids. When the team was on the road, the Laker wives hosted watch parties at one another's houses so that we could cheer on our husbands as a group. When new players joined the team, the veteran wives welcomed the new wives into the fold, helping them settle into our city by inviting them to our team family functions and hipping them to everything from which schools would be great for their kids, to the best neighborhoods to live in, to the coolest places to shop. None of us would let so much as a week go by without us getting together, supporting one another, and saying, "If you need anything, let me know. We have people." We shared babysitters, tutors, hairstylists—the works. The bond the Lakers wives shared was even more special because most of the players tended to stay on the team, so we got to know one another and become longtime friends; we were loving families, united.

This was the precedence set by the coach. Pat Riley was leading the team at that time, and because he had a stellar relationship with his wife, Chris, the two worked together to make sure we couples stuck together, too. Truly, Coach Riley believed that when his players had strong home lives, their game stayed strong, too. Jerry West, the general manager, and his wife, Karen, operated in pretty much the same way; he would encourage the players to depend on the bonds they shared with their wives and children for motivation and strength, and she would organize fund-raisers and more personal get-togethers with the wives so we could bond as families—together.

Coach Riley believed that when his players had strong home lives, their game stayed strong, too.

Beyond that, I had no time for champagne tossing anyway; I was much too busy being a mother. Though my sister was nearby and pitched in when I needed help with the baby, caring for our newborn son while Earvin began forging a path as a commentator, business owner, and HIV advocate was, like for most mothers, a full-time job. Despite that both Earvin's mother and my own didn't believe in letting someone else "raise the baby," I did hire a live-in nanny because I needed the help, but I was a hands-on mom who did a lot of the heavy lifting on my own during the day, and all of it at night, as I felt staying up with EJ was my responsibility. Even when Earvin was home, rarely did he change diapers, feed the baby, or wake up when our child cried throughout the night, so full-time care fell squarely on my shoulders. I was so exhausted from caring for our son one night that I literally ran into a wall. EJ was crying in his bassinet by our bed, and nothing—not a feeding, not a diaper change, not soft talking or singing—could soothe him. At my wit's end, I picked him up for what seemed like the fiftieth time and held him against my chest as I walked and rocked and shushed him some more; Earvin, completely oblivious to the chaos, kept right on sleeping, no doubt helped along by my leaving the light off. Thing is, while sleeping in the dark worked just fine for Earvin, it didn't bode well for a sleep-deprived, heavy-eyed, dog-tired new mom: as I walked in circles with EJ, I slammed against the wall.

"Oh my God, I can't do this anymore!" I yelled, bursting into tears. My wail was as loud as the baby's.

Earvin, startled by the racket, finally woke up. Rubbing his eyes, he swung his long legs over the side of the bed and rushed over to me. "Get in the bed," he said, taking the baby from my arms. "I got the baby. We're good. Get some rest."

It was an early-morning wake-up call that snapped Earvin into dad duty. Though my breastfeeding kept him from being able to feed our son in the earliest months, when he was home, Earvin, ever the early riser, would take the 4:00 a.m. shift so that I could rest.

When we adopted Elisa and brought her home, the nanny helped me juggle my duties with our children so that they both felt like they were getting the attention they needed and deserved. While the nanny bathed one child, I would read to the other; if I was up late with Elisa, the nanny would drive EJ to preschool while I caught up on my rest. But I never shirked my responsibilities as a mother, devolving into the stereotypical role of an aloof celebrity mom who leaves the rearing of her kids in the hands of "the help" while focusing on "me time" and running behind her husband. I was deeply involved in their lives and enjoyed my role as their mom. I fed them, dressed them, researched which schools they should attend, sat through parent-teacher conferences, volunteered at school events, cheered them on in plays, recitals, and sporting events, chauffeured them to doctor appointments, worried about them, loved them, prayed for them. I poured everything into my children because I relished being a mother much more than I wanted to run around trying to be seen in the Hollywood lights.

My kids needed that attention—craved it. Both were diagnosed with attention deficit disorder, and while their chronic condition didn't stop them from being amazing kids, it did add to the challenge of raising them. Elisa's behavior really put my mothering skills to the test, as it manifested itself in a hyperactivity and impulsiveness that, on some days, would bring us all to the edge.

I remember the ruckus she raised one night while Earvin and I hosted an adult party in our backyard. Elisa was only about three and a half, but she wanted to be the center of the action. "No, baby, it's eight o'clock," I said, giving her a kiss and putting her into the nanny's arms. "It's bedtime. Mommy will be right outside. Get your rest."

I was outside talking and laughing with our guests when, not fifteen minutes later, the nanny tapped me on the shoulder. "I don't know what to do, Miss Cookie," she said, looking harried.

"What do you mean? What's wrong?" I asked, worried.

The nanny gestured for me to follow her back into the house; Elisa was at the door, crying and screaming her head off. Terrified, I took her into my arms. "Oh my God, what's wrong?" I asked. Elisa pointed her tiny finger outside, toward the tennis court, where our guests had gathered. "Oh, no no, baby, you have to get your rest." Rubbing her back, I rushed her upstairs and promised her I'd be the one to give her a bath, but after that, she'd have to go to bed. This only made her more angry, and before I knew it was coming, my daughter, her body shaking in rage, took my hair in both her little hands and pulled as hard as she could while she let out a rebel yell that bordered on a scene from *The Exorcist*.

"Elisa! Stop it!" I yelled, trying to wrest my hair from her tiny hands. Somehow I managed to get this little ball of anger and energy into the bathroom, where the nanny had already run her bath, but the second her little pinky toe hit the water, she started a fresh round of screaming and banged on the glass shower door like she was trying to break it, raging so hard I thought maybe her little eyeballs would pop out of the sockets. She flipped out all through her bath, while I got her into her pajamas, and again when she realized I was heading toward her bed. She was determined to get her way. This incident, along with several other breakdowns and, later, some overbearing, bossy ways with some of her friends at school, made it clear that our daughter was dealing with something bigger than a strong will. By the third grade, I noticed the signs—how she couldn't sit still in class, how short an attention span she had while doing work, and how, even at home, we had a hard time getting her to sit for dinner. She would take a couple bites, then flip around the room, stopping only to grab another bite or two and then go back to flipping. After going through virtually the same thing with EJ, I knew she was probably suffering from ADD. Her mind functioned really well; she just needed a little something to calm her down. I found a great educational therapist to teach her how to organize herself in a way to get her work done, and she was fine. Being there for her, paying attention, and working hard to help her manage her emotions was tough, but it was a challenge that I put my full heart into because she is my daughter and I am her mother. It is what good moms do.

Motherhood trials got even more complicated when Earvin's HIV status was added to the mix. The personal shunning I'd feared became a reality after I had children, like the one time during a playdate EJ bit the son of one of my friends. Now, this isn't anything unusual for toddlers; they bite and hit when they can't find the words to express their anger or frustration. In other words, EJ was simply being a kid when he chomped on my friend's child. Well, you should have seen the look of terror on my friend's face! She ran over screaming, "Oh my God!"

Right away, I knew what she was afraid of. "Calm down," I told her. "EJ doesn't have the disease. You don't have to worry."

She was relieved but still worried about long-term implications. "I'm so glad you brought that up," she said. "Do I need to take my son to get a shot or something?"

I reassured her that her son was fine.

My friend's reaction was hard to take, but I understood it. Her Momma Bear instincts had kicked in; if the shoe had been on the other foot, I might have had the same reaction. Earvin and I just had to learn to live with the fact that no matter how much other people learned about HIV, and no matter how friendly others seemed when they were with us, they would probably always be somewhat standoffish and uncomfortable. Most people were too polite to act like they were scared of us—but I'm sure many of them secretly were. It hurt to keep that in the back of my mind as my children and I interacted with the people we knew and loved.

Parenting while my husband rebuilt his empire sometimes felt like a solitary job, and rearing our children in a celebrity culture of excess came with its tests, but, thankfully, our tiny clan was attached, too, to a mix of close friends and an extended family that provided the right kind of reinforcements we needed to keep EJ and Elisa grounded. Once a month, for instance, the kids participated in get-togethers with a group of like-minded African American friends—our own Jack and Jill society of sorts to help the kids bond with one another over their similar experiences. Understand, it's not that I didn't want my kids to have white friends; it was a given that they'd have pals that crossed racial lines, seeing as that is who was mostly in the private schools they attended. But we'd been around black children who grew up with so much excess and exclusiveness that they couldn't identify with people who looked just like them. Some didn't want to. Earvin and I didn't want that to be our children's story, so, from the time they were little, we paired them with a core group of black families with children who were like-minded in that they appreciated and respected their heritage. These kids spent a lot of time together, at barbecues, sleepovers, the movies, and the park. To this day, these are the kids they trust and love. That makes me feel good; it's important to me that they understand their heritage and that they avoid pretending to be something they're not. I wanted them to have that cultural balance.

Economic balance was important to us, too, and we achieved that by making sure our children stuck to the roots that kept Earvin and me grounded. Every year, from the time EJ was fifteen months old, Earvin and I would take a two-week vacation together while the kids stayed with our families in Detroit and Lansing. One week, they'd be at Earvin's mom's house, with all his brothers, sisters, and their children, and then they would drive up ninety minutes to Detroit to my mom's, where they'd stay with my brother, his son, and the neighborhood kids they got to know over their yearly visits. This was the equivalent of my going down South, back to Alabama each summer—a trip that was meant to remind us where we came from and who was important in our lives. Earvin's sister Pearl, with whom I'm really close, would take the kids on trips around Lansing, and then all the rest of his siblings would take turns doing the same. Then, in Detroit, my mother played the big kid when EJ was on the scene: she was the expert on the video games and would play Super Mario better than her grandson and his friends. So good was she that EJ's friends would always call and ask, "Can your Grandy tell us how to beat this monster?" It would be one big playdate at her house.

To this day, my kids can identify with it all—their blackness, humble roots, family ties that bind. Sure, EJ shines as a cast member on *Rich Kids of Beverly Hills*, a reality show about the young adult children of wealthy celebrities, but it is much more of a stepping-stone for him to become a talk show host than it is a public display of our wealth. EJ and his sister were raised with intention, and they're putting all that Earvin and

I taught them during our parenting journey to good use. I'm proud of that.

· Doing My Own Thing ·

Beyond being a mom and wife and using my philanthropic plat-form alongside Earvin's to advocate for women, children, and those affected by HIV and AIDS, I've had my own ambitions and managed to bring one of my biggest ideas to fruition: CJ by Cookie Johnson, my line of premium denim jeans. I'm so proud of what I accomplished with the brand; being a part of the fash-ion industry had been a dream of mine since I was a young girl, enamored by modeling and fancy clothes. In fact, I wanted to be a model when I was little, and my mother even indulged that pas-sion by signing me up for classes with Barbizon, an agency that taught modeling and etiquette to young hopefuls. My father hated every moment of it; he thought the program was a money-suck, and maybe it was. In addition to class fees, we students had to buy a cabinet full of makeup and a closet full of clothes, plus pay for a photo shoot and the shots it yielded. We ended up putting out much more money than I earned back. Still, I picked up some valuable tips from those classes: proper grooming, like how to pluck my eyebrows and apply makeup; how to walk; how to pull together outfits for different occasions; how to sit properly and hold a conversation; how to walk a runway and pose for pictures.

I loved the class—particularly the sessions that focused on styling. There was something about running through the department store, pulling clothes for the different looks—business, playful, evening, formal—that was captivating, irresistible. I still have those "modeling" pictures; they're hilarious. Every time I pull them out, I crack up at my J. C. Penney clothes. I really thought I was something else. I can't say I loved the modeling part—I was tragically shy and couldn't pull my nerves together to make a go of a career as a professional fashionista. I would do just fine in front of the camera, but when it came to strutting the catwalk in front of an audience, I would freeze and come this close to fainting when it was my turn. But the Barbizon experience opened my eyes to the business side of fashion and convinced me to pursue it as a career as early as high school, when I attended a trade school that specialized in fashion and design. There, I got hands-on experience picking out patterns, judging which fabrics were best for specific styles, and sewing entire outfits. I loved it so much, I decided then that I wanted to study fashion in college and focus my career on being a buyer. I earned a bachelor of science degree in retailing of clothing and textiles. Starting my own clothing line was a natural extension of that, and in 2009, after years of planning, strategizing, and putting in an ocean's worth of sweat equity, I debuted my jeans.

The concept for the line was deeply personal and incredibly simple: I wanted to create aspirational jeans for women with curves. The fashion industry labeled curvy as plus size, but that's not what "curves" meant to me. I wanted a line of premium denim that would fit women shaped like me, with small waists and round hips and butts. I'd always had a time finding jeans that fit; if they were sized for my waist, they were too snug in my hips and behind, and if they fit in those areas, the waist felt like a hula hoop—way too big. I'd be in fitting rooms disgusted and murmuring to myself: "I am not huge! I am not this obese woman! Can I find at least one pair of jeans that I can get over my thighs? One?" By the time I finished getting my jeans tailored to fit my proportions, I'd end up spending double the cost others paid for their denim. This, I knew, was the plight of not only mostly black women, but other women, too, who tend to be shaped like Coke bottles: small waists, ample elsewhere. My goal was to create a line that would appeal to and fit them.

It was—and remains—a stellar concept, one that the creator of the Rich & Skinny premium jean line immediately understood and agreed to help me set up. He already had the infrastructure: a factory and warehouse based in Los Angeles, and years of experience and know-how marketing and promoting his über successful brand, which made it that much easier for me to establish my own line. He brought the organization, and I brought my style and celebrity, plus a friend, a former buyer for Nordstrom, who agreed to walk my brand into the department store with the hope that they would carry my line there. With an initial investment, I agreed to split the profits equally with my new partner, with CJ by Cookie Johnson as a specialty brand under his line; we then got to work designing and creating my jeans in October 2008, with the intention of debuting it during All-Star Weekend in February 2009.

This was no easy proposition: getting a line designed, constructed, placed in stores, and properly marketed in four months was a Herculean effort as it was, but forcing non-traditionally-cut jeans into a fashion industry that tended to ignore the needs of women who fell outside of the waiflike ideal made things that much tougher. For starters, we had the hardest time simply finding what is known in the industry as a "fit model," meaning a woman whose proportions represent the typical pattern and sample size for the jeans. At first, I thought my team was stalling because I insisted on hiring a black model, but after weeks passed by, finally, they came to me and broke the news: "We can't find one."

"What do you mean you can't find one?" I asked.

As it turns out, black fit models literally did not exist because no one made clothes for the body type my designer was cutting the pattern for. The typical fit model has thin thighs and a flat butt, the exact opposite of what we needed. It took us weeks to track down a black model who fit the bill, and even she had to do squats and leg lifts to fill out the samples we had in mind.

Finding a curvy black fit model would turn out to be the least of our worries. My team warned me that I couldn't call CJ by Cookie

Johnson a "black line," because mainstream stores wouldn't want to stock it, and magazines would not review or cover it. It would be cursed, too—ignored, or, worse, buried in the plus-size section—if the jeans had a tagline that mentioned the word "curvy." Though my denim went from sizes four to eighteen, we certainly weren't plus-sized, but having that stamp, my team warned, would relegate my jeans into the missy departments where clothes considered dated, frumpy, and unattractive went to die. I understood the challenges, but describing my jeans as "curvy" fit with the mission, so I ran with it—to our detriment. Sure enough, countless magazines refused to feature the line in their pages, and the few who bothered to write about it did so only in editorials about plus-size denim or makeovers for heavy women who lost a little weight. To this day, it remains the same—the most frustrating thing ever, particularly considering we're in an age, now, where bodacious derrieres and tiny waists are leading a modern-day fashion renaissance, with celebrities such as Kim Kardashian, Jennifer Lopez, Iggy Azalea, and the like leading the public charge for women with curves. When women try on my jeans, they get it: they understand the difference, and they love that a designer put some thought into how the cuts and styles fit their particular body type.

I know they changed the way I wore jeans. I was skinny before I had EJ, but after I gave birth, my body morphed into a curvy wonder that no longer fit comfortably into the jeans I already owned. It was the worst: all of a sudden, they were super snug on my hips, and my rounder butt made my jeans sit way lower on my body, exposing much more skin than I cared to show. I would wear long sweaters in ninety-degree weather to avoid flashing butt crack while sitting in chairs with open backs or squatting to play with my son at the Mommy and Me classes.

But my new jeans changed the game. The first customer tried on a pair at the debut launch at Nordstrom, during the NBA All-Star Weekend. She was screaming before she could get out of the dressing room: "Oh my God! It went up over my thighs *and* fit my waist!" Without a belt. She ran around the store twirling and squatting. "Look, I can bend over!" she said excitedly. My partner just laughed and laughed. I invited my friends to come down to try on a few pairs, too, including some of my fellow basketball wives. "Wow, I can't believe it," I heard over and over again.

Then one lady, a total nonbeliever, walked over. She was sharp: in her late forties, cute, wearing a crisp shirt, black stretchy pants, and these really cool platform shoes. Her purse was perfection, as were her makeup and jewelry. She would be, I decided, a perfect tester. "Are you going to try on the jeans today?"

"I don't wear jeans," she sniffed.

I knew why: she wasn't fat, but she wasn't small, either, and she had a bit of a booty, even for a white woman. "No, you have to try these," I insisted.

"I know, the sales girl called me," she said. "But jeans never fit me, so I don't bother. I just came in to see you."

I literally took her by the hand: "Please, just come in the dressing room and try them on for me."

Finally, she relented. While the woman tried on the jeans, I stood at the front of the dressing room, talking to friends and helping others pick styles to try. After a while, I noticed that the reluctant woman hadn't come out, and I began to worry. I knocked on her dressing room door: "Are you okay? What's going on? Did they not fit?"

Slowly, she opened the door and there she stood, teary-eyed. "I can't believe they fit." She turned to show me her backside; the jeans fit her like a glove. She took off prancing around the dressing room, dancing and jumping and saying, "I cannot believe this!" Her happiness made me cry, too. She was confirming what I already knew: that my jeans were sewn with a smidge of self-esteem in the seams—a fit that allowed curvy women who thought they'd never be able to wear jeans to feel sexy in denim.

We started the line modestly, getting them placed in ten Nordstrom stores, and then I went on a desk-side tour, bringing samples and pitching the line to as many magazine editors who would see me. One of those editors was the creative director at *O*, the magazine owned by Oprah Winfrey. The stakes were high, there, because at the time, Oprah still had her television show, and if she so much as mentioned your product on *Oprah* or featured it in her magazine, the chances were that it would experience what became known as the "Oprah Effect," meaning that, with the power of her clout, your product would sell through the roof. I wanted it—badly. Her creative director wouldn't make any promises, but he made clear he understood the concept and would do what he could to get the jeans on *Oprah*. "They'll be good for her," he said, "because I know she was having a hard time trying to find jeans that fit. I dress her for the covers all the time, so I'll reach out and have you send over her size and we'll see."

Not long after, we sent over the boyfriend jean, and he called to let me know that Oprah had actually tried them on. That's all he had for me then, but two weeks later, I got a text from Gayle King, the magazine's editor and Oprah's best friend, that Oprah loved the jeans and wanted to know if she could keep them. "What?" I answered back quickly. "Yes! Let her take them home!"

I was on cloud nine with the news but still unsure if anything would come of it. Another week passed by before I found out for sure that she would wear CJ by Cookie Johnson on the cover. Shortly after that, an *Oprah* producer called to ask if I would fly into New York to tape a segment about my jeans for an upcoming show.

I promise you, I didn't know what to do with myself; I was beyond ecstatic. Earvin and I were on a college tour with EJ when I got the call; the show flew in a team to interview Earvin and me just as we were planning to take EJ for a visit to NYU, and then, two days later, we flew to Chicago for the in-studio session with Oprah. Talking to her about my jeans was surreal; there I was, this woman who'd dreamed since she was a little girl of being in the fashion industry, sitting on the stage of a seminal show, with the most important pop cultural phenomenon on the planet, talking about clothing I'd created. That dream I'd dreamed—that passion that burned in my heart from junior high through college and broken engagements and a high-profile marriage and a huge health crisis and two kids and all the drama that came with it all—was finally a reality.

The "Oprah effect" translated into my line going from ten Nordstrom stores to virtually all of them, plus placements in Neiman Marcus. My base customer fell between the ages of thirty and fifty and usually wore a size twelve. We had a pretty good run, too, with the jeans selling well enough for me to be able to afford my own overhead and turn a nice profit. But later, after the publicity from the Oprah appearance died down, it became difficult for my customers to find the jeans in the stores. Women would come up to me all the time saying, "I love your jeans! I found a pair a while ago, but why can't I find them in stores now? Where do I get them?" I had no answer for them, really. I made a solid product, but the stores still didn't know what to do with a jean line designed for curvy bodies.

If there was one thing I wished I could have changed about the experience, it was the price point. My jeans were premium quality and made in America, which meant the material and labor cost more, and that cost got passed on to the consumer, who had to pay upward of two hundred dollars for a pair of CJ by Cookie Johnson jeans. I would have loved for the price point to be lower, but building a more affordable line would have required me to set up operations in China, which, I found out early on, was impossible because someone overseas had trademarked the CJ by Cookie Johnson name and wanted me to pay a ridiculous amount to get it back. This, I found out the hard way, was a common practice in China—one that my first partner and I didn't take seriously because we were so focused on building a premium brand. But later, when I was looking to revamp the line, that mistake of failing to trademark overseas came back to haunt me.

Still, I'm proud of what I built. I had a son in high school, a daughter who'd just started junior high, and a husband who was off forging his own way with his businesses, and I managed to keep up with my responsibilities for my family and honor my own desire to have a career. Earvin was incredibly supportive; when I told him about my plans, without hesitation, he said, "I know you've always wanted to do this, so do it." I was proud of myself because I found a way to start my own company without saying, "Honey, can I have some money?" I struck my own deal, I set my sights on what needed to be done, and I got to it. That tenacity, mixed with an unshakeable faith I had in myself to balance home and true career, is what real basketball wives are made of.

Chapter Eleven

In This Life Together

Forever. That's what Earvin and I promised to pour into our marriage—a happily ever after built on a foundation of love, mutual respect, and family. We'd done a good job of it, too, considering the challenges, which came at breakneck speed almost before we'd had any real chance to unpack from our short honeymoon. But a decade into our marriage, *forever* started to crack and bend under the pressure that came with distance—an emotional and physical void that had slowly grown as Earvin found his footing with his foundation and business, and I deep-dived into the raising and rearing of our kids. The truth is, after all the fighting we'd done to be and stay together, a different kind of fight was forcing us apart.

I didn't notice it at first. I was knee-deep in parenting our children, who'd both been diagnosed with attention deficit disorder, which required a separate level of care that extended far beyond my typical mom duties. Between school, educational therapist appointments, extracurricular activities, and shuttling them all over town, I wouldn't get home until well after seven o'clock in the evening, and once we arrived, I'd throw myself into the whirl-wind of dinner, homework, and bedtime rituals that would keep me going full speed until after nine o'clock. By the time I laid my head down at night, Earvin, who goes to bed super early, would be long asleep, making intimacy and the connection we needed as husband and wife, not just parents and friends, a no-go. We talked very little, and when we did, it was mostly logistics: "EJ's birth-day is coming up, what day do you think we can have his party?" and "The pediatric neurologist thinks the new medicine will help Elisa focus. I'm thinking about putting her on it." Then, we'd go to sleep and wake up the next day and go our separate ways again, acting like nothing was wrong but clear, in our hearts, that everything between us was off.

And that was when my husband was actually home. Though he'd long retired from the NBA and the hectic schedules that came with playing professional ball, Earvin's time was being monopo-lized by his new team, the group of women and men he'd hired to help him run Magic Johnson Enterprises, his burgeoning empire of movie theaters, restaurants, coffee houses, and health clubs. Of course, I understood the pull; Earvin was working hard to build a legacy—a successful company that would not only create a family fortune but also leave a footprint of entrepreneurship across the urban landscape, which was thirsty and primed for the businesses that traditionally avoided the very neighborhoods Earvin was serving. It was, and is, a noble, lucrative venture. Still, somewhere in the midst of the building, he pulled away from home. Rather than spend time with the kids and me, he was going out for after-work business meetings, parties, and get-togethers with his employees and business partners, who also happened to be a troupe of women who were as beautiful as they were intelligent. I'd be exhausted and harried, giving baths and reading books to the kids, trying to get them down for the night, and Earvin would be in the bedroom, getting dressed to go play cards or have dinner with his employees. "But you went out yesterday and a couple nights ago, too," I began saying more than I wanted.

"I'm just going out with the team, Cookie," he would insist. "I'm building this business."

As that particular conversation increased its frequency, so did the angry tone and tenor, until, finally, our talks got explosive. I hated that he was leaving the kids and me behind, even going so far as to give up the planning of family vacations—something he'd always enjoyed—no matter how hard I tried to coordinate them with his busy schedule. "Are you coming?" I would ask, exasperated, as departure day drew near. "Well, you guys go ahead and I'll meet you there," he'd say. He did that a couple times, and then a few vacations after that, he didn't show up at all. One year, he traveled with us, and then, a few days in, ditched our family trip to attend the Essence Music Festival, an annual conference and music event for women. That one really stung, not only because his leaving felt like he was ignoring our children, but also because I couldn't understand why he would skip taking me, his wife, along with him to a festival he knew I would enjoy.

"Well, you already planned the vacation," he said, trying to explain why he didn't think to bring me to the Essence Music Festival with him.

"Because you didn't tell me you were going to the festival!" I argued.

And then we would fight. This was our way, stretching for at least three years.

The fights between Earvin and me felt familiar—would put me right back to what it felt like to listen to my parents argue when I was but a small child in Alabama, and later in Detroit, when I was older and understood a bit better the impact their relationship trouble would eventually have on our family. One of their arguments was so explosive that I remember it to this day, even though I was only about five. My sister and I were in our room sleeping when their muffled voices grew louder and louder still, until, finally, my parents' bedroom door flung open, slamming against the wall, and those voices roared against the walls and straight to our room. My mother ran in first, my father fast on her heels. I can't recall at all what they were arguing about, but I can still see their eyes squinty and red and filled with rage, and I especially remember how loud my heart beat when my mother grabbed a baton my sister and I would play with and waved it in my father's direction, trying hard to connect that metal with his head, back, shoulders—whatever she could. "Mommy!" my sister and I screamed, trying desperately to get her to drop the weapon. But they kept right on yelling at each other, my father's voice a deep rumble, my mother's a screeching, feisty shriek. It's funny: when I look at the two of them today, I can't imagine them fighting like that, but they were so different when they were younger and quicker to let their tempers and passion override the feelings that made them fall in love. Just as scary as the verbal sparring was the emotional gymnastics they'd employ for days after the big fight: my mother would retreat into a shell of silence, refusing to speak to my father, who would, in turn, use us to communicate with her. "Tell your mother the heater needs adjusting and I'm going to fix it after I get off work," he would tell us, with my mother sitting right there, within earshot, pretending like she was ignoring us all.

"Tell your father I said fine," she'd say back.

They had their good times, of course, and those memories dance around in my mind, too—how my father would tool around on his Harley, in his tattered leather jacket and his cut-off blue jeans with the flag on the back. One night as they got ready to go out, my mother broke out an outfit that was white leather, head to toe—the jacket, pants, boots. She put on her helmet, got on that motorcycle, and wrapped her arms around my father's waist, and the two of them sped off, the motor of the bike revving, the smiles on their faces spread cheek to cheek. They were sharp together and when they were happy, the sun danced. But when they fought, it was awful and scary and made the kid me want to disappear beyond the storm—to run somewhere back toward the sun, where there was peace.

There was no peace in our home when Earvin and I were going through our relationship troubles, either. This much was clear: our marriage was strained. Very. And every problem we'd left to fester under the surface finally came to a head one evening in 2001, during a huge party Earvin had planned to celebrate his star on the famed Hollywood Walk of Fame. All our friends were there, as were the employees from his office, and my husband was making a point of entertaining all of them while I sat off to the side, upset. Granted, it was our way to go our separate ways at functions such as these; we didn't need to be attached to the hip. But eventually, we would always find our way back to each other, especially when the music started playing and the dance floor filled. Always, we would dance together. But on this night, that didn't happen; I was annoyed and my husband was off dancing with the pretty women from his office and also another group of women I'd seen around but didn't know. They were dancing very close—familiar. I didn't like it. Perhaps it meant nothing to him, but at that moment, when I was already emotional, it was a big deal—the straw that broke the camel's back. I found out much later that those girls really were just employees and acquaintances, but in that moment, it looked like something I needed to question. I marched up to Earvin and got in his face: "I'm here and you're just going to ignore me?" I asked, near hysterics in the middle of the dance floor. "Is this what you're doing when you're going out all the time and I don't know where you are?"

Understand, this was totally out of character for me. Never once in our relationship did I question who he was with and what he was doing with them, let alone do it in a crowded, public space. But I needed him to understand that we were at a critical point in our relationship, and if I was standing there calling him out, we had a serious problem and he would have to, for the sake of our relationship, respect that I needed him to stop what he was doing and focus on me.

Earvin did no such thing. "Just go sit down," he said, seething. The woman with whom he was dancing just stood there, boldly looking on but refusing to leave. "I'll be with you in a minute," Earvin insisted.

"What?" I said, incredulous. "That's how you're going to play this? She needs to go sit down, and you need to come with me, your wife."

"What? Go sit down!" he yelled, every ounce of ultra macho leaping from his throat. Earvin had never been one for ultimatums; that night was no exception, and his stance made clear that instead of understanding just how upset I was, he was going to double down. "You're not going to stand here fronting on me in front of all my guests!"

It was getting to be a scene with the people dancing around us. Before our conversation turned into an all-out screaming match on the dance floor, my friend, Sharon, came over and grabbed my arm. "Let's go," she said, tugging me away. "We're going to the bathroom. Come with me."

Embarrassed, angry, and feeling completely disrespected, I dissolved into a heap of tears in that restroom. My friend wiped my tears and sat and listened without judging. Then, when I asked that she get me out of there, she piled me into her car and took me home. I wanted no part of Earvin—didn't want to see his face. When I got home, I paced and worried and stared at the pile of suitcases in our bedroom; we were scheduled to go on a family vacation the very next day—a vacation that Earvin had actually planned—and I had not one clue how we were going to be around each other for two weeks when we were so mad at each other.

Later that night when Earvin arrived home, he came straight to the kitchen looking for me. He didn't bother with greetings or niceties. "We need to talk," he said. And as if the bell had been rung in a heavyweight-boxing match, the fight was on.

"You totally disrespected me, and I can't believe you were dancing with those girls while I tried to talk to you and asked you to come with me!" I yelled. "I felt completely disrespected, and that's not right!"

"You feel disrespected?" Earvin snapped. "You disrespected me. How you gonna come out there and snatch my arm and tell me to come with you? Don't you ever do that! As a matter of fact, we got serious problems here. So here's what we're going to do: after this vacation, we're going to see how we get along and then we're going to make the decision on whether we're going to stay together."

His words sent a shockwave through my body. For years, we'd both seen the sign, lit like neon lights down our marital path, and we were slowly, surely, sputtering

His words sent a shockwave through my body.

toward it: divorce. But I didn't know we were that close to the end. "Wow. Fine," was all I could muster.

That next day, we left for the Atlantis resort in the Bahamas and ended up having a pretty decent time, considering. But after almost five days in, just when I thought that we were heading toward reconciliation and primed to talk about ways to fix what was broken, Earvin cut his part of the trip short. "I'm leaving," he said simply. "By the time you all get back to LA, I'll have moved out."

I was devastated. "We're not going to try to talk about this? This is it? This is just the way it's going to be?" I asked, tears flowing. "What went wrong? Is it another woman? What's going on?"

"No," he said quietly. "We don't talk anymore. We don't spend any time together anymore, and we just don't connect anymore."

"But we can work on this," I insisted. "Please, don't do this."

"No. I'm done."

In shock, I couldn't think of anything else to say. Clearly, he'd made up his mind and, in all the years that we'd been together, I knew that once this man settled on his direction, there was no changing course. "Okay," I said. "Fine. Go."

The next day, that's exactly what he did. Unbeknownst to me, his people were already at our house, packing up some of his clothes and other things he needed to live on his own. Our children kept asking, "Where did Daddy go?" I played it off as best I could: "He went out of town." For all they knew, their daddy was away as usual on one of his business trips—everything was normal. I needed them to think that. Honestly, I didn't have the heart to tell them we'd broken up or that their father was leaving me. Plus, I thought it unfair that I'd be left holding that bag; if Earvin truly was going, he would have to explain his decision, not me.

When the kids and I arrived back home two days later, Earvin was living with his son Andre in his four-bedroom apartment across town. He'd actually moved out, and that stunned me. Earvin hadn't even mentioned the "D" word—divorce—but being separated was overwhelming. I tried to keep myself busy to stop my mind from wandering back to our breakup, but in the quiet moments, when the kids were away at school or at night after I'd read them their books and tucked them into bed, my heart was absolutely broken. I was broken. The only thing that could even remotely pull my pieces together was my children— their voices, their laughter, the patter of their feet as they ran through the house, oblivious to the pain that pulsed through my body from the break of morning till the second I closed my eyes at night. When I wasn't crying or trying to keep myself busy, I was consumed with pondering how, exactly, I was going to raise our babies and live the rest of my days without the love of my life. I had no idea how I would move on—or if I could.

How did I get through it? The same way I always had: I took it to the Lord and put it in His hands. I started that process in my Bible study group, with my sister and my girlfriends, who, stunned by the news, got into prayer-warrior mode and helped me fall to my knees and reach out to God. They were such a huge comfort and stayed in my corner—no judgment—while I got myself together and ready for battle.

Understand, when I say "battle," I don't mean I was spoiling for a fight. I was preparing for spiritual warfare. As a Christian, my focus was more on listening for God's direction. Rather than wait for Earvin's call, I humbled myself and asked the Lord not to fix my marriage or bring Earvin back home, but to show me how to survive the relationship—whatever He willed it to become. Morning, noon, night, my prayer was the same: "Lord, Your will be done. You are the head of my life and my focus is on You.

Whatever You want for me, I accept it." And with that, I pulled myself together and made plans to spend a few days at a spa in Arizona with my girlfriends, to take a break, clear my mind, recuperate from the trauma, and focus on pulling myself together.

Nearly a week had passed by, and Earvin didn't bother to call; I gathered he was busy with whatever or whomever he was running to. But I thought it important to let him know I was leaving the kids with the nanny while I traveled to Arizona, so I called him. "I just need to get away, kick back, and relax for a minute," I explained. "The kids are in good hands. I just thought you should know."

"Well, while you're gone, I'll come over and watch the kids," he offered, to my surprise. "When you come back, I'll leave."

"That'll be fine," I said, keeping our discussion cordial and quick.

And with that, I went my way and Earvin went his.

· Is This the End? ·

I hadn't expected Earvin's call the day I was heading back to Los Angeles after my spa retreat, but there he was on my cell phone, trying to coax me into joining him and the kids for brunch with some friends of ours—couples with whom we always hung out. "When you come in, why don't you have Donald take you to the restaurant, and then we'll all go home from there."

The offer confused me. Plus, after a few days of stewing over Earvin's disappearing act, the last thing I wanted to do was to sit in front of our kids and close friends and pretend everything was cool and normal. "I'm not going anywhere with you," I said simply.

"No, come on. It's no big deal," he insisted. "We're just having brunch with the kids."

"Well, did you tell them that we're not together anymore? Do they know that?"

Earvin took a beat. "No, I haven't," he said. "When we come home, we'll sit down and get the kids together and talk to them."

"Okay, that sounds like a plan," I said. "But I don't need to go to brunch. I'm just going to go home. I'm fine." And with that, I hung up.

Almost as quickly as we said "bye," Earvin called back. "Cookie, come on and go with us to brunch. I think you should come. Everybody's asking for you."

I frowned at the phone, trying to figure out why Earvin was so insistent that I come hang with him and the kids. My girl-friends, who over the prior few days prayed with me and also willed Earvin to go jump in a lake for hurting me, all of a sudden were pushing me to attend that family brunch. "Go, go, go!" they insisted, egging me on.

And so I did. And when we sat at that table, our children and friends surrounding us with love, it almost felt normal again—

like that groove Earvin and I and our family always had. One by one, the men came my way and folded me into their embrace as they looked into my eyes and pledged their support. "You're not going anywhere. Nobody is going anywhere." Clearly, Earvin had told them what happened, and just as my girlfriends had my back, his friends had his. Ours. I got super emotional because it was so sweet; here they were, rooting for us to get it together. "Whatever the problem is," they said, "you both need to figure it out." Earvin just sat there, grinning. I hadn't a clue what he was plotting and planning, but I was alternately warmed and confused.

Later that evening, when Earvin brought the kids home, he waited downstairs while I got the kids to bed. I fully expected that once they were down, he would leave. But Earvin had other plans. "I thought maybe I'd stay tonight," he said.

"No, you're not doing that," I said, adamant. "We're either together or we're not. But what I won't be a part of is confusing our kids. Did you even talk to them?"

"No," he admitted.

"You're coming back tomorrow to tell them, right?"

"Yea, but I should just stay here," Earvin insisted. "It's late. It would be better if I stayed."

A little more probing and I got to the bottom of what Earvin was really trying to say: he wanted to move back in and work out our relationship. "Absolutely not," I countered. I wanted no part of the Magic Roller Coaster and, frankly, I was mad he'd forced me into the front seat of his crazy ride. The truth is that while I wanted to be with my husband, I couldn't see myself being in a marriage that took me outside of who I was—a marriage that made me question and wonder and worry about who my husband was with and where he was and what he was doing. I had never concerned myself with such things, and now it was making me crazy. And that could only lead to me making my husband crazy. As hard as it would have been for me to say good-bye to our marriage, it would have been a relief to me to have the space to be the woman I am, instead of the wife I was becoming. I have to admit, though: I was relieved to know that the short time Earvin was away made him realize what he had.

Finally, he agreed to leave but promised he would be back the next day—and he was, making that same pitch, except this time, with some explanation for what, exactly, was going on in his head in the first place. "I don't know what got into me. I thought I wanted something else or that I needed to be out there on my own, but when I got out there, I realized that wasn't what I wanted."

"But you were only out there for two weeks," I said. "How could you figure all that out that quickly?"

"I knew," he said quietly. "I just knew. I woke up in that bed and asked myself, 'What are you doing? This is stupid. This is not where you're supposed to be.' I want to come home."

I have to admit, I needed more than a chorus of, "I miss you and the kids and I was wrong." I needed some assurances that instead of pretending like the prior two weeks didn't happen, we would go back through three years' worth of baggage, figure out where we both went wrong, and then work hard to fix what truly was broken. "We have to figure this out, and I'm thinking we need to go talk to somebody," I said.

Thankfully, he agreed. We started by talking to our pastor, whom we trusted to give us an honest, no-holds-barred plan for how to get back to what God intended for the two of us. We also talked to our trusted friends—couples who knew us well, honestly wanted the best for us, and had valuable advice on how they made their love and trust last through the years. One of them gave me a book that, to this day, I believe made a big difference in our marriage. *The Power of a Praying Wife*, by Stormie Omartian, not only taught me the power of prayer focused specifically on marriage but also helped me to understand that I had to step back and let God control the situation. I appreciated the lessons on how to build up my husband and support him so that he could be the head of the family, as he should be. That's not an easy thing for a strong woman to do, sure. But, as the book instructed, doing so will earn his respect and encourage him to build up his wife as God guides him. Ultimately, I learned, God is the head of your marriage.

Armed with encouragement from our pastor and friends and the work I did based on that book, finally, Earvin and I talked with each other, confronting head-on our issues and making promises that we would work individually on the things that would make us stronger as a couple. He complained that I'd been so focused on the kids that I no longer *saw* him. "There's no room in there for me," he said. What's more, he was bothered that I wasn't taking care of my physical self the way I'd been before we had kids, and he wanted me to recognize that keeping myself up was important to him. What did I need from him? Assurances that while he grew his business, he wouldn't put his work before his family. Of course, I understood that he was excited about his company because it was growing rapidly, and I respected that for him to perform as a businessman at the same level as he did on the court, he needed to rally himself and pump up his team much like he did when he was a professional baller. But he needed to understand that the rallying needed to include his significant other. In other words, I needed to be included not so much in the business, but certainly in the social aspects that helped the team to gel together. "If you're having a card party, a barbecue, or a dinner with your crew, you should be bringing your wife. You can't keep compartmentalizing to the point where you're leaving me out of the most important parts of your life," I said. "That's not what you do in a marriage."

By August, we were on the good foot, working toward fixing us. To show his pleasure with our recommitment to each other and to thank me for sticking by his side, Earvin rented part of the Magic Mountain amusement park and planned a huge tenth-anniversary party, with one hundred guests. Everybody was there—all the family and friends who loved us and wanted nothing but the best for our marriage. We picnicked together and played carnival games while our favorite tunes by Maze featuring Frankie Beverly, Earth, Wind & Fire, and Luther Vandross blasted from the massive speakers around the park; I even went on a roller coaster or two, though I did that with my friends, because Earvin is not a fan of riding them. Later, after all the fun, we had cake. It was there, among the roller coasters, cotton candy, and whirl-a-twirl rides that Earvin stood up in front of everyone and made an emotional speech professing his dedication to our union. Though I can't remember the words verbatim, I do remember the sentiment behind them: they were every bit as poetic as they were beautiful, and they served not only as the pitch-perfect apology for the drama he brought to our doorstep but also as an assurance that he was with me and the kids for the long haul, no matter what.

We made a lot of promises to each other during that reconciliation period and, thankfully, gratefully, it stuck. We focused on the little things—leaving the kids home while we went out on dates. Friday night was our night; we went to movies, out for dessert, and had easy, simple moments that helped us really connect. Earvin also started taking an active role in being involved with the everyday inner workings of the family, chipping in with shuttling the kids to birthday parties on the weekends, planning our vacations, and really enjoying spending time with me and the kids during our travels. Now, when he was planning, he was including us more. He and I also started taking an annual month-long cruise with our married friends, during which we sail, eat, shop, and bond across Europe. It is in those moments, big and small, that we reminded ourselves why we were together and why we needed to stay together. It wasn't about money. It wasn't about celebrity. It wasn't about fast women and loose morals and some kind of failure to keep it in check. It wasn't about sticking with what we knew—what we were comfortable with. Stripped down to the bone, our breakup was about a man and a woman, a husband and a wife, a mother and a father, and the effects the typical seven-year itch had on the love we had for each other. By the end of it, we'd made an agreement that became a turning point in our marriage: no matter what we were going through or how difficult it became, we'd always talk about it. *Always*. And that is a promise that we've kept.

· *The Story of Us Continues* ·

Twenty-five years later, here we stand, Earvin and I, in this new chapter of life, having fought our way to love. No one ever said love would be easy. But ours is a love story for the ages—a real-life example of a committed long-term relationship that is neither ordinary nor fairy tale, but worthy of exploration and celebration. Together we've battled a deadly disease and overcome a seemingly insurmountable, career-ending social stigmatization that tested our allegiance to each other. We raised our children in the whirlwind of celebrity, nursing them through health and social challenges of their own, and, in the process, managed to fortify our hearts and recommit to each other as man and wife, even when we thought we'd fallen apart forever. Two and a half decades of commitment is nothing to sneeze at. Since we said "I do" in that Lansing, Michigan, chapel on that fine summer day in 1991, we've seen the invention of the internet, the devastation of global terrorism and war, the cloning of animals, and the election of the first African American president. And through it all, Earvin and I have remained together, a testament to practicing what we preached at the altar: for better, for worse, for richer and for poorer, through sickness and in health, 'til death do us part. For Earvin and me, being together—staying together—is as important as breathing air. It is not an option. It is what we do. Because a promise is a promise. Because we love each other.

Being married under the conditions we faced was challenging, and, of course, there were times when, exhausted and confused, we questioned just how in the world people stay married, raise families, and keep hold of who they truly are in the process—all without resorting to hand-to-hand combat. But for us, the glue that binds is our abiding faith, a trust that God never gives us more than we can handle, yes, but also that He brought Earvin and I together for a much larger purpose. We have seen this manifest itself not only in our lives and those of our children, but in the larger societal context that came when Earvin announced he was HIV-positive. For nearly a quarter of a century, Earvin has been the heterosexual face of HIV. Since the day he walked through our front door and told me he was infected, I've stood by his side. I've held him up. I've loved him. And even when we were going through our issues as a couple, I have believed in him. God insisted on that. As a result, in the years following Earvin's announcement, it seemed like everyone was thinking more deeply about how one could contract HIV, understanding that it is neither solely a gay disease nor solely a drug user disease, but an illness that can be contracted by all humans, no matter the lifestyle, sexual choices, wealth, or access to treatment. Through Earvin's story, millions have been reached, and some are alive today because he stood in front of the world, bared his soul, and encouraged anyone who could hear his voice to get tested, practice safe sex and, if infected, take their meds.

Amazingly, in the midst of Earvin's journey, I, too, found my voice and joined my husband in the HIV advocacy space. As a Magic Johnson Foundation board member, I've worked tirelessly to spread the word to women in general and women in urban populations in particular about the importance of getting tested, protecting themselves, and empowering themselves to make choices about their sexuality that positively impact their lives. Black women, after all, are among the most vulnerable group— more than three times as likely to be diagnosed with HIV than their white counterparts. Though a Centers for Disease Control and Prevention analysis shows that new diagnoses among African American women fell a whopping 42 percent between 2005 and 2014, there is still plenty of work to be done to reduce the numbers further. I take great pride in the work I did as part of the "I Stand with Magic" campaign, our foundation's quest to help reduce new infections in our community by fifty percent. Though I've never been comfortable in the spotlight, I pushed past the nervousness of speaking in front of audiences to participate in HIV and AIDS discussions in churches, schools, and community programs across the country, encouraging women to demand safe sex and work hard to take care of themselves as passionately as they care for their families. In lifting my voice to empower women, I gained some strength of my own.

Some people's attitudes about HIV and AIDS have changed; chalk that up to the improvement in drug treatments, which have led to those who have the virus living longer. But there is still plenty of work to do, and we recognize that we have to remain diligent. To this day, I still run across those who believe you can contract the virus just by touching someone. And when it comes to fighting the spread of the disease by encouraging the use of condoms, there's still so much work to do. This is still a disease that can kill. It's not something to play with. We know we can't let our guard down.

Twenty-five years ago, if you would've told me that God would somehow use this devastating disease to lead us both toward the work He wanted us to do, I would've thought you were crazy. But our biggest heartache has been our greatest gift. It gave us a sense of purpose. And for that, I will be grateful. Always.

Now that my kids have gone off to college and started lives separate and independent of the ones we built for them under our roof, I've gotten more involved in my husband's foundation. If I accomplish one remaining thing during my time on this earth, I want it to be educating others about HIV and AIDS. There doesn't have to be an epidemic. We can dramatically reduce the number of new cases by always educating ourselves, using protection and getting tested, and by urging our friends and loved ones to do the same.

On a more personal level, as Earvin and I reflect on our twenty-five years of marriage and look forward to twenty-five more, I want us to continue to be a solid foundation for each other, and an example of committed love—the kind that slams up against modern day notions that there is something wrong with marriage. Pop cultural attitudes and headlines obscure another reality: that there are many more couples just like us—happy, in love, dedicated, and committed. The best Earvin and I can do is prove the statistics wrong by keeping our eyes on each other and focusing on all the good that comes with being in this life together. For ourselves. For our children. For our community. For love.

We're going to make it.

· Acknowledgments ·

Extending love and honor to my parents, Cora Kelly and, in loving memory, Earl Kelly, who taught me everything.

To my loving husband, Earvin, who supports me in all my endeavors and loves me unconditionally: thank you for believing in me.

To my children, EJ and Elisa, both of whom I love dearly: thank you for the joy you've brought to my life. Thank you, too, for being my stylists and always keeping me looking current and up to date.

To my sister, Pat: thank you for spending long hours with me helping to put this book together. I couldn't have done it without you.

To my assistant, Aneesha Saleem: thank you for keeping us all coordinated and on point.

To Denene Millner, the most amazing writer: thank you for understanding exactly who I am.

Thank you Alex Glass, my literary agent, for convincing me that I could do this.

Thank you to Howard Books for believing my story was important.